And Then Some

Dr. Randy Johnson

All Scripture references are from the New
International Version, unless noted.

Published by:

RM Rochester Media

© 2010 Randy Johnson

Published by:
Rochester Media LLC
P.O. Box 80002
Rochester, MI 48308
248-429-READ
www.rochestermedia.com

All scripture quotations, unless otherwise indicated, are taken from Holy Bible, New International Version NIV ® copyright © 1973, 1978, 1984 by International Bible Society.

Author: Dr. Randy Johnson
Cover Photography and Design: K Woodard Graphics
First U.S. Edition Year 1st Edition was Published

Summary: Why the Savior went above and beyond what was required?

ISBN: 978-1451542677

1. Christian Living, Spiritual Growth, Christianity, Religion

For current information about releases by Dr. Randy Johnson or other releases from Rochester Media, visit our website: http://www.rochestermedia.com

Table of Contents

Introduction

"You're fired!" Those words have been quoted regularly since 2004 as individuals mimic Donald Trump. Basically, it is just three words. You are fired! However, those three words are life-changing, life-altering words for many people. Three words can break a groomed professional.

"I love you!" Again, just three words, but so much more. Three words that everyone needs to hear. Those simple words hold hope and promise. In addition, it should be noted that the opposite expression, "I hate you," also holds heart-wrenching power.

This book is about three words. Three words. Just three words. Three one-syllable words. Words that can and should change the course of one's life.

The difference between the ordinary and the extraordinary Christian lies in just three words: *And Then Some.* These words contain the mindset to do more than expected. *And Then Some* is just that little extra more than ordinary. That little difference can mean more than one could ever realize.

Habit number two of Steven Covey's book, *7 Habits of Highly Effective People,* encourages individuals to write a mission statement for their life. It helps to begin with the end in mind. I believe an effective mission statement could be just three words long: *And Then Some*.

In fact, Jesus even held a mission statement for His life that was stitched with *And Then Some*.

Throughout this book I have inserted pictures of crosses that I have in my office. Although the cross symbolized a horrible death in the first century, today it means new life and eternal life for believers. I also use the pictures to lead to the conclusion of this book.

CHAPTER ONE - DOWNWARD

GOD TO US

*"The next day Moses entered the Tent of
the Testimony and saw that Aaron's staff,
which represented the house of Levi,
had not only sprouted but had budded,
blossomed and produced almonds"*
(Numbers 17:8).

God Almighty doesn't deal with ordinary people in simple ordinary ways. He is a God of the Extra Ordinary. In Numbers 17 God displays His willingness to go over and above the call of duty. Korah's rebellion caused immense confusion and complaining throughout Israel. A battle over leadership had surfaced. So, God set up a test to distinguish whom He had chosen to lead Israel. The staff belonging to the man He chose would sprout. One leader from each of the tribes of Israel picked a staff, wrote his name on it and gave it to Moses. Moses then placed the staffs before the Lord in

9

the Tent of the Testimony. The next day when Moses entered the Tent of the Testimony he immediately spotted Aaron's staff. Yes, Aaron's staff sprouted. However, it more than sprouted. In just one night it sprouted, budded, blossomed and produced almonds! God had agreed to perform a miracle so the people would realize the leader was truly chosen by Him. God not only spoke through the miracle, He shouted. He had the staff sprout - *And Then Some*.

In 2 Chronicles chapter one, a pinnacle scenario takes place in the life of Solomon. Solomon went up to the altar before the Lord and offered a thousand burnt offerings. Solomon offered a thousand burnt offerings. One Thousand! However, the conversation to follow is so amazing most everyone forgets the offerings. Verse seven reads, "That night God appeared to Solomon and said to him, 'Ask for whatever you want me to give you.'" This appears to be a dream where one finds a lamp, rubs it and a huge genie appears. Solomon is asked by God Almighty to share his number one wish. It appears Solomon has thought about this position and is immediately ready to give an answer. He asks just for wisdom. Solomon's response pleases God.

Verses eleven and twelve reveal God's practice of blessing far above what is humbly asked. "God said to Solomon, 'Since this is your heart's desire and you have not asked for wealth, riches or honor, nor for the death of your enemies, and since you have not asked for a long life but for wisdom and knowledge to govern my people over whom I have made you king, therefore wisdom and knowledge will be given you. And I will also give you wealth, riches and honor, such as no king who was before you ever had and none after you will have.'" God gave Solomon wisdom and money *And Then Some*.

Likewise, Jesus constantly displayed the attitude of giving a little more. Sometimes in discussing the life of Jesus it is profitable to start with His death. Jesus died for us ... *And Then Some*.

It should be remembered that Jesus came to earth to die. He lived to die. Our sin had broken connection with God. The only way our relationship with God could be restored was through a perfect sacrifice. The only suitable sacrifice was God's only son. So, from our perspective, Jesus had to die. Philippians 2:5-8 points out how Jesus died and yet did so much more:

"Your attitude should be the same as that of Christ Jesus: Who, being in very nature God, did not consider equality with God something to be grasped, but made himself nothing, taking the very nature of a servant, being made in human likeness. And being found in appearance as a man, he

humbled himself and became obedient to death—
even death on a cross!"

Jesus only needed to die. Yet, he chose to humble Himself. He died as a common criminal. He chose the cross. Jesus did more than expected. Romans 5:8 points out that Jesus died for us while we were sinners: "But God demonstrates his own love for us in this: While we were still sinners, Christ died for us." It makes more sense to die for a family member or a dear friend than to die for those who are your enemies. Jesus truly died for His enemies. Jesus died for sinners. He didn't have to, but He chose to. It wouldn't surprise us to have a mother die for her child. Children even speak of being willing to die for the dear family pet. Men have always been known to fight for their families. But Jesus did more. Jesus died for us.

Not only did Jesus die for sinners, but He chose the humblest of means. He chose the cross. It should be noted that the cross was the fulfillment of prophecy. Psalm 22 describes Jesus' death in graphic detail one thousand years before it was to take place. Amazingly, the Messiah's crucifixion was described years before anyone experienced or even knew of this means of execution. Jesus could have written prophecy to have Himself die a heroic death. Yet, he chose the cross. Instead of people cheering, Jesus heard them mocking and felt their spit and fists. Men dream of dying the heroic death. In war films, the hero dives on the live grenade or jumps in front of a speeding bullet. Jesus chose the cross. Movies often display examples of heroic sacrificial deaths:

In **John Q**, Denzel Washington plays the part of a father who is willing to lay down his life for his son.

In **Armaggedon**, Bruce Willis allows himself to get nuked to destroy the asteroid hurtling toward earth. All praise him as he goes back to "press the button."

In **The Bodyguard**, Kevin Costner dives in front of Whitney Houston to take a bullet. He doesn't die, but his sacrificial move is classified as purely heroic.

Jesus didn't want the glory. Jesus chose the cross. Jesus chose an extraordinary humble death. Interestingly, the events of His life piece together an extraordinary humble life.

Poverty: Samuel Clemens, better known as Mark Twain, has been quoted as saying, "I am opposed to millionaires, but it would be dangerous to offer me the position." It is pretty fair to assume that just about anyone would choose to be rich if it were an option. Jesus had the choice. He could have come to earth in total royalty, but He chose to relate to those who struggle financially.

It all started with Jesus' birth. Jesus chose to be born in the most humble circumstances. Luke 2:4-7 says, "So Joseph also went up from the town of Nazareth in Galilee to Judea, to Bethlehem the town of David, because he belonged to the house and line of David. He went there to register with Mary, who was pledged to be married to him and was expecting a child. While they were there, the time came for the baby to be born, and she gave birth to her firstborn, a son. She wrapped him in cloths and placed him in a manger, because there was no room for them in the inn." Be it a barn or a cave, Jesus chose to relate to those who aren't born with silver spoons in their mouths.

Sheldon Danziger wrote the article on poverty for the

2004 World Book Encyclopedia. He states, "Poverty is the lack of enough income and resources to live adequately by community standards." He goes on to state that even though it is difficult to determine standards from country to country, there are over one billion people that are "so poor that their health and lives are endangered." One billion people equate to about a sixth of the world's population.

God has always cared for the poor. Leviticus chapter twelve gives special instructions for the poor concerning offerings. After a woman gave birth to a child, she had some steps to follow. Part of the process involved a burnt offering and a sin offering. A year-old lamb is needed. However, verse eight makes a provision for the poor, "If she cannot afford a lamb, she is to bring two doves or two young pigeons, one for a burnt offering and the other for a sin offering. In this way the priest will make atonement for her, and she will be clean.'"

Luke 2:21-24 describes Jesus' earthly parents as poor. "On the eighth day, when it was time to circumcise him, he was named Jesus, the name the angel had given him before he had been conceived. When the time of their purification according to the Law of Moses had been completed, Joseph and Mary took him to Jerusalem to present him to the Lord (as it is written in the Law of the Lord, 'Every firstborn male is to be consecrated to the Lord'), and to offer a sacrifice in keeping with what is said in the Law of the Lord: 'a pair of doves or two young pigeons.'" Walter Liefeld writes, "The

offering of birds instead of a lamb shows that he was born into a poor family. Perhaps this helped him identify with the poor of the land." Joseph and Mary couldn't afford a lamb. Jesus identifies with us by choosing to be born into a family that couldn't even afford a lamb for the offering. Yes, He relates to those who live paycheck to paycheck.

Even in Jesus' adult life it is recorded that He lived a life of poverty. In Matthew 8:20 (repeated in Luke 9:58), the author states, "Jesus replied, 'Foxes have holes and birds of the air have nests, but the Son of Man has no place to lay his head.'" There would be nothing wrong with Jesus having a palace and living a comfortable lifestyle. Money is not evil. 1 Timothy 6:10 does not say that money is evil. It is the love of money that poses the problem. It appears that Abraham, Job, David, Solomon, Joseph of Arimathea and Lydia were godly individuals who were wealthy. Jesus had every right to own a house, have servants and never miss a meal. But, He chose to relate to the bulk of humanity. David Allen points out that one-sixth of Matthew, Mark and Luke, and twelve of Jesus' thirty-eight parables have to do with money. Jesus realized that money was perceived to be a big deal, so He refused to let it become the deal. He chose the simple life. He relates. He knows what it means to struggle. Jesus came to die for us, but He also came to live for us, like us ...*And Then Some*.

On the move: How often do people move in their lifetime? Using 2007 ACS data, it is estimated that a person in the United States can expect to move 11.7 times in their lifetime based upon the current age structure and average rates and allowing for no more than one move per single year. At age 18, a person can expect to move another 9.1 times in their remaining lifetime On the average, this would mean

people move about once every seven years. There are a lot
of variables involved, but it is safe to say that
people are on the move.

People seem to always be on the move. Making new
friends seems to be a common problem. Families have moved
away from their extended relatives and rely on strangers
to help raise their children. Moves can be difficult on all
involved especially children. In 2003 a remake of the movie,
Cheaper by the Dozen, hit the screen. Steve Martin plays
the part of the father who takes a new coaching job in the city. A
central theme of the movie shows how difficult moving can
be on the children. Again, Jesus chose to relate to us.

Matthew 2:13-15 states, "When they had gone, an
angel of the Lord appeared to Joseph in a dream. 'Get up,'
he said, 'take the child and his mother and escape to Egypt.
Stay there until I tell you, for Herod is going to search for the
child to kill him.' So he got up, took the child and his mother
during the night and left for Egypt, where he stayed until the
death of Herod. And so was fulfilled what the Lord had said
through the prophet: 'Out of Egypt I called my son.'"

Right after His birth, Jesus and His family were on
the move. Jesus' move was a little more unique than most as
His life was in jeopardy. Herod was set on killing all the baby
boys in Jerusalem. Hence, Joseph packed up the family and

headed at least seventy-five miles south. Jesus didn't really get to know his grandparents. He wasn't raised playing with His cousin John. The only family He really knew were His parents and step brothers and sisters. Jesus came to die for us, but He also came to live for us, like us ...*And Then Some*.

Reputation: In **The Scarlet Letter**, Nathaniel Hawthorne describes the after effects of an affair between Hester Prynne and the minister, Arthur Dimmesdale. The affair resulted in the birth of a daughter named Pearl. Pearl was teased, mistreated and avoided by the other children. She was an outcast because it was known that she was an illegitimate child. This was not her choice, but it was her life. Jesus could relate. He chose to relate. We can imagine that other children teased Jesus. It was well known that Mary was pregnant before she married Joseph. Even more, imagine what children would say when Jesus or His family talked about His virgin birth. He would be target number one for insults. Children can be cruel. Adults can be cruel. Jesus chose to relate to victims. Jesus came to die for us, but He also came to live for us, like us ...*And Then Some*.

Minority: I have been Youth Pastoring at Chinese Churches for over ten years. I often joke that I am a minority among minorities. Although I may joke, I can't fully relate to minority status. But Jesus can. Jesus chose to come to Earth when Jews were under servitude to the Romans. He didn't come when it was good to be Jewish. He chose slavery. He chose to be the victim of prejudice and racism. The majority of people can't relate to being a minority. Jesus can. He knows what it is like to be a minority. Jesus came to die for us, but He also came to live for us, like us ...*And Then Some*.

Blended family: Joseph was His stepfather. Think about that! Someone may argue that Christ's birth was inevitable, and He couldn't be born of man due to sin nature. However, He didn't have to be born. God created Adam as a grown man. He created Eve as a grown woman out of Adam's rib. He could have chosen to come to earth as an adult, die, resurrect and go back home to Heaven. It could be one busy week. But He chose to relate. He came as a baby, grew up and lived a perfect, sinless life. He chose 33 years of relating to everyday life including the blended family. Our earthly father or stepfather may not understand us, but Jesus does. He relates. Jesus came to die for us, but He also came to live for us, like us ...*And Then Some*.

Wrong side of tracks: I was raised less than a mile north of Detroit. Detroit often has the reputation of "The Murder City" as opposed to "The Motor City." When I was younger, it was fun watching the response of people when I was on vacation. People would ask where I was from. I would say, "Detroit" or "The Detroit area." Fear and panic became commonplace. Often people felt sorry for me. Typically, in my experience, people wouldn't choose to be from Detroit. Here too, Jesus could relate.

In John chapter one Jesus calls His disciples to follow Him. John 1:43-46 says, "The next day Jesus decided to leave for Galilee. Finding Philip, he said to him, 'Follow me.' Philip, like Andrew and Peter, was from the town of Bethsaida. Philip found Nathanael and told him, 'We have found the one Moses wrote about in the Law, and about whom the prophets also wrote—Jesus of Nazareth, the son of Joseph.' 'Nazareth! Can anything good come from there?' Nathanael asked. 'Come and see,' said Philip."

Jesus could have been from any city. He could have chosen Rome or Athens or even Jerusalem, but He chose Nazareth. Nazareth is not even mentioned in the Old Testament. There was nothing special about Nazareth. Nazareth was like the wrong side of the tracks. R. L. Alden points out that the modern area of Nazareth has only one spring. Nazareth was not listed in the Old Testament, Talmud or ever by the historian Josephus. Nazareth was very possibly an insignificant town. People knew of Sepphoris, the larger city to the north. But Nazareth was nothing. It would not have been chosen for the Olympics, Super Bowl or an All-

Star Game. It was just Nazareth. It was known for nothing. Would people know of Nazareth? Nazareth was nowhere.

Nathanael was ready to write Jesus off simply based on the fact of what city He was from. Merrill Tenney points out that Nathanael may have viewed Nazareth as a rival village. It may have been poorer or morally worse than his town, Bethsaida. Nazareth could have been viewed as a welfare town or even "sin city." What would people think today if we heard that Jesus was from Las Vegas? Jesus was perfect, but He didn't care about image. He cared about relating. He related to everyone because He cared. He was Jesus of Nazareth. Jesus was from nowhere special. He could have chosen a popular, famous city, but He again chose to be overly normal. Jesus came to die for us, but He also came to live for us, like us ...*And Then Some*.

His appearance: When I was in ninth grade I prayed every night for two things. First, that my older sister, who was mentally retarded, would become normal. Vicki is two and a half years older than me. When she was fifteen months old she acquired encephalitis and medically died. She is still alive, but only has the mind of an eight-month old. I prayed regularly that she would be normal again. Second, I prayed that I would be 6 foot 3 ½ inches tall. I loved basketball and thought 6'3 ½" was perfect. It is sad to admit that one of my

most important prayer requests was to change the way God made me. My vain thought patterns were not unique to me.

In fact, cosmetic surgery statistics are alarming. According to the American Society for Aesthetic Plastic Surgery (ASAPS) there were nearly 11.9 million surgical and nonsurgical cosmetic procedures performed in 2004. People have a variety of choices. They can have liposuction, breast augmentation, eyelid surgery, rhinoplasty, Botox injection, laser hair removal and facelifts. If given a choice, many people would change something in their appearance.

Wayne Rice of Youth Specialties reported that actress Michelle Pfeiffer appeared on the cover of a magazine with the headlines "What Michelle Pfeiffer Needs Is ...Absolutely Nothing!" A reporter discovered later that Michelle needed over $1,500 worth of touch-up work on the cover shot. The artist's bill gave the following list as items that were done to make Michelle Pfeiffer appear even more beautiful than she was: "Clean up complexion, soften eye lines, soften smile line, add color to lips, trim chin, remove neck lines, soften line under earlobe, add highlights to earrings, add blush to cheek, clean up neckline, remove stray hair, remove hair strands on dress, adjust color and add hair on top of head, add dress on side to create better line, add forehead, add dress on shoulder, soften neck muscle a bit, clean up and smooth dress folds under arm, and create one seam on image on right side." The total price was $1,525.00. It is funny that someone who needs absolutely nothing needed so much. It is also a reminder that the most beautiful people in the world wish they looked as good as they are often portrayed. They too have features they would change.

1 Samuel 16:7 points out that humans are overly conscious of outward appearances. "But the LORD said to Samuel, 'Do not consider his appearance or his height, for I have rejected him. The LORD does not look at the things man looks at. Man looks at the outward appearance, but the LORD looks at the heart.'" People often judge the book of one's life by the outward cover.

Jesus is the only man who could choose exactly how He wanted to appear. He could have been absolutely beautiful, yet he chose to relate to common folk. Isaiah 52:2 paints His image: "He grew up before him like a tender shoot, and like a root out of dry ground. He had no beauty or majesty to attract us to him, nothing in his appearance that we should desire him." There was nothing in His appearance that we should desire Him! He didn't obtain beauty or majesty to get our attention. Jesus wasn't striking. He wasn't gorgeous. He was plain, simple common folk. People passed right by Him without ever noticing His normal look. Jesus chose to be like us. He didn't have to, but still He did it. Most people would have chosen to be dessert to the eye, the envy of all, and the dream come true. But not Jesus. He went over and above the call of duty and chose to relate to us. Jesus came to die for us, but He also came to live for us, like us ...*And Then Some*.

Despised: Often, when a celebrity comes to town, a big welcome party is thrown. There are banners and the marching band leads the parade. Jesus deserved such a welcome, but He didn't receive one. Isaiah 53:3 states, "He was despised and rejected by men, a man of sorrows, and familiar with suffering. Like one from whom men hide their faces he was despised, and we esteemed him not." Jesus was despised. He wasn't welcomed. Many of us can relate to walking into a room and realizing that we weren't wanted. We want to be loved and appreciated. Jesus would have enjoyed those feelings, too, but He was despised and rejected. It wasn't just at His death that He felt unwanted.

Early in Jesus' ministry He came home to preach. Mark 6:2-3 gives the response of the people, "'Where did this man get these things?' they asked. 'What's this wisdom that has been given him, that he even does miracles! Isn't this the carpenter? Isn't this Mary's son and the brother of James, Joseph, Judas and Simon? Aren't his sisters here with us?' And they took offense at him." The people didn't give Jesus a warm reception. There was no welcome-home party. They took offense at Him. He was despised and rejected.

Later during the Triumphal Entry, Mark writes in chapter eleven verse eighteen, "The chief priests and the teachers of the law heard this and began looking for a way to kill him, for they feared him, because the whole crowd was amazed at his teaching." Jesus was so despised that people wanted to kill Him. He wasn't accepted in His homeland and He wasn't accepted by religious leaders. There is not much one can do when he isn't accepted at home or at church.

Luke 22:63-65 states how the guards treated Jesus, "The men who were guarding Jesus began mocking and beating him. They blindfolded him and demanded, 'Prophesy! Who hit you?' And they said many other insulting things to him." The guards mocked Jesus and insulted Him. People who didn't even know Him found their place in despising Him. Jesus can relate to the mindset that feels "if they really knew me they would like me." But they didn't. They mocked and insulted Him.

It is horrible to feel unwanted. We like to be liked. It is typical for people to over-analyze why they are not liked. We wonder if things would be different if we did something different. We don't like being left out, ignored or avoided. Jesus chose to relate. He was despised and rejected.

Matthew 26:67 is disturbing, "Then they spit in his face and struck him with their fists. Others slapped him." They hit Him, slapped Him and spit in His face. Spit! They spit in his face. I don't think there could be a greater insult. They spit in His face and He allowed it. In every way, Jesus chose to relate to us *And Then Some*.

The Message Bible paraphrases Isaiah 53:3, "He

was looked down on and passed over, a man who suffered, who knew pain firsthand. One look at him and people turned away. We looked down on him, thought he was scum." The New Life Version is consistent with this thought, "He was hated and men would have nothing to do with Him, a man of sorrows and suffering, knowing sadness well. We hid, as it were, our faces from Him. He was hated, and we did not think well of Him." Jesus was treated as scum because He was hated. Jesus came to die for us, but He also came to live for us, like us ...*And Then Some.*

Temptation: One of the most common stories of Scripture shows Satan tempting Jesus. In Luke 4 Satan tempts Jesus to turn the stones into bread. That would be quite a temptation after fasting for forty days. He then bribes Jesus with all the eye can see. Finally, he tries pride. He challenges Jesus to jump from the highest point of the temple. Of course the angels would catch the Son of God. In each situation Jesus quoted Scripture and stood strong. Jesus didn't have to allow Himself to be tempted, but He did allow it. He allowed it so He could better relate to us, show His perfection through it all, and set an example for us to follow.

1 John 2:16 states that the three areas in which Jesus was tempted are common to us. "For everything in the world—the cravings of sinful man, the lust of his eyes and the boasting of what he has and does—comes not from the Father but from the world." Eve saw the fruit, knew it would taste special, and wanted the wisdom it would bring. David saw Bathsheba's beauty, desired her, and demanded her presence. He knew she was married, but he was the king.

A great reminder is stated in 1 Corinthians 10:13, "No temptation has seized you except what is common to man. And God is faithful; he will not let you be tempted beyond what you can bear. But when you are tempted, he will also provide a way out so that you can stand up under it." First, our temptation is common to all. Our backgrounds and financial statements may be unique, but temptation is common. Second, we can never say, "The Devil made me do it." He doesn't have that much control. God offers victory every time. In Genesis 39, victory for Joseph meant running out of a room. In Genesis 45, victory meant meeting his brothers face to face and forgiving them for selling him into slavery.

Jesus chose to experience temptation like each of us, yet He teaches us to pray that we would not experience temptation. The Lord's Prayer in Matthew 6:13 reads, "And lead us not into temptation, but deliver us from the evil one." Jesus wants us to avoid tempting situations. He could have avoided it, but He didn't. He experienced temptation and won every time.

Hebrews 2:18 is so encouraging, "Because he himself suffered when he was tempted, he is able to help those who are being tempted. " Jesus was tempted so He knows the feeling. He can empathize. "For we do not have a high priest who is unable to sympathize with our weaknesses, but we have one who has been tempted in every way, just as we are—yet was without sin" (Hebrews 4:15). Jesus not only died for us, but He lived every day for us. He lived a sinless life for 33 years and then died in our place. Yes, Jesus came to die for us, but He also came to live for us, like us ...*And Then Some*.

CHAPTER TWO - DOWNWARD

GOD TO US

And Then Some – **And Even More**

"The thief comes only to steal and kill
and destroy; I have come that they may
have life, and have it to the full"
(John 10:10).

A s a child I acquired a poor theological concept that controlled a lot of my thinking. I wasn't taught this dogma at church or home. I just developed it in my own mind without realizing it. I believed that you had only two choices: One, you could accept Christ as Savior and have eternal life in Heaven when you die, but life on earth would be miserable; or two, you could reject Christ and go to Hell when you die, but have a blast on earth and get the most out of every day until death. It was either Hell on earth and Heaven forever, or Heaven on earth and Hell forever. I was afraid to give my life totally to God because then He would send me to the place I didn't want to go, doing the thing I didn't want to do. It wasn't until I grew older and wiser that I realized my theology was common, but wrong. Actually, Jesus offers Heaven and abundant life. Rejecting Christ leads to Hell and a void in one's daily walk. Jesus offers a win/win situation.

I think John 3:16 is the cake, and John 10:10 is the icing. John 3:16 is the most famous verse in the Bible and it reads, "For God so loved the world that he gave his one and only Son, that whoever believes in him shall not perish but have eternal life." The foundation of Christianity is solid on the promise of salvation through Jesus Christ. Our sin broke our relationship with God. He offers reconciliation through His Son's death. This reconciliation brings eternal life. John 10:10 gives the bonus of daily blessings, "The thief comes only to steal and kill and destroy; I have come that they may have life, and have it to the full." Not only do we get eternal life and Heaven, but we also are offered life to the full. Jesus offers us abundant life. There are at least four passages that emphasize aspects that comprise abundant life. These are offers from God that all would desire.

Comfort

People often say that becoming a Christian would be so much easier in the first century, and that it would be easier to live consistently as a Christian in the first century. Seeing Jesus and being right with Him would cast out all doubt. However, this isn't accurate. Jesus limited His deity so that

He chose to only be in one place at a time. When He left, He sent the Holy Spirit to be with believers at all times. We receive comfort with His indwelling us. Jesus' leaving was to our advantage. John16:7 says, "But I tell you the truth: It

is for your good that I am going away. Unless I go away, the Counselor will not come to you; but if I go, I will send him to you." It sounds out of place to hear Jesus saying that it is for our good that He went away. After He left the earth, He sent the Holy Spirit back to His followers.

John 14:16-17 reads, "And I will ask the Father, and he will give you another Counselor to be with you forever— the Spirit of truth. The world cannot accept him, because it neither sees him nor knows him. But you know him, for he lives with you and will be in you." Jesus gave us a Counselor to be with us all the time. We often go through times when we need comfort. So, Jesus gave us the Holy Spirit.

God comforts us in all of our troubles. 2 Corinthians 1:3-4 says, "Praise be to the God and Father of our Lord Jesus Christ, the Father of compassion and the God of all comfort, who comforts us in all our troubles, so that we can comfort those in any trouble with the comfort we ourselves have received from God." God comforts His children. He is the loving Father.

Safety

God is always watching His children. In Psalm 139:7-12 David describes the Lord's omnipresence, "Where can I go from your Spirit? Where can I flee from your presence? If I go up to the heavens, you are there; if I make my bed in the depths, you are there. If I rise on the wings of the dawn, if I settle on the far side of the sea, even there your hand will guide me, your right hand will hold me fast. If I say, 'Surely the darkness will hide me and the light become night around me,' even the darkness will not be dark to you; the night will shine like the day, for darkness is as light to you." God is always with us. Nothing can happen to us without His permission. Job chapter one shares a discussion between God and Satan. Satan complains that Job only serves the Lord because he is blessed. Satan goes on to point out the safety net Job has in verse 10, "Have you not put a hedge around him and his household and everything he has? You have blessed the work of his hands, so that his flocks and herds are spread throughout the land." Satan realized that God put a hedge around His child Job. God then gives permission for Satan to try Job's faith. Realize, Satan had to get permission. David confidently speaks of God's protective hand in Psalm 27:1-3, "The LORD is my light and my salvation— whom shall I fear? The LORD is the stronghold of my life— of whom shall I be afraid? When evil men advance against me to devour my flesh, when my enemies and my foes attack me, they will stumble and fall. Though an army besiege me, my heart will not fear; though war break out against me, even then will I be confident." Confidence comes in the Lord.

David continues this thought as he draws a clear visual in verse five, "For in the day of trouble he will keep me safe in his dwelling; he will hide me in the shelter of his tabernacle and set me high upon a rock." When little

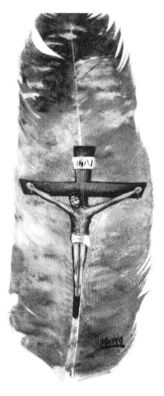

children are going to visit, it is good to "child-proof" the house. Everything of value is placed out of reach of trouble. Likewise, God finds value in His children, so He places them out of reach of trouble.

There are so many times that God protects us without us ever realizing it. Bad traffic, delays, and set backs should be viewed as God's way of having us avoid a disaster. God is watching out for us. God has our back. Psalm 23 comforts us as verse four records, "Even though I walk through the valley of the shadow of death, I will fear no evil, for you are with me; your rod and your staff, they comfort me." We need not fear because "You are with me."

Finally, a common life verse is Jeremiah 29:11, "'For I know the plans I have for you,' declares the LORD, 'plans to prosper you and not to harm you, plans to give you hope and a future.'" It is not in God's plans to harm us. He gives hope and a future.

Needs Met

"The LORD is my shepherd, I shall not be in want" (Psalm 23:1). Phillip Keller, author of A Shepherd Looks at Psalm 23, states, "What a proud, positive, bold statement to make! Obviously, this is the sentiment of a sheep utterly satisfied with its owner, perfectly content with its lot in life." My needs are met because the Lord is my shepherd. Keller continues, "No doubt the main concept is that of not lacking – not deficient – in proper care, management or husbandry." Jesus calls Himself our shepherd. In John chapter ten He defines part of His role as our shepherd. In verse eleven

He says, "I am the good shepherd. The good shepherd lays down his life for the sheep." Jesus would do anything for us, including dying for us. He again refers to Himself as our shepherd in verse fourteen, "I am the good shepherd; I know my sheep and my sheep know me." Keller later says, "When all is said and done the welfare of any flock is entirely dependent upon the management afforded them by their owner." Knowing Jesus is our shepherd, we should, "Come, let us bow down in worship, let us kneel before the LORD our Maker; for he is our God and we are the people of his pasture, the flock under his care" (Psalm 95:6-7). The Lord is our shepherd. We should worship Him. We are not in need. David opens Psalm 23 saying we don't have unmet needs and closes with, "Surely goodness and love will follow me all the days of my life, and I will dwell in the house of the LORD forever." The child of God should experience goodness and love. The Lord is our shepherd.

Strength / Peace

The Lord offers salvation and so much more. David again captures part of the promises of life to the full for the children of God, "The LORD gives strength to his people; the LORD blesses his people with peace" (Psalm 29:11). Strength and peace are part of the abundant life.

The Lord gives strength to His people. Every day should be started by seeking the Lord's strength. Paul realized that fear can be reduced and even eliminated by accepting the Lord's strength. He wrote in Philippians 4:13, "I can do everything through him who gives me strength." The Lord gives strength to His people.

The Lord also gives His people peace. Peace has two aspects. Romans 5:1 shows that salvation brings peace with God, "Therefore, since we have been justified through faith, we have peace with God through our Lord Jesus Christ." We are no longer at war with God. We now have peace with Him. Second, once we are saved, we also experience the peace of God. Philippians 4:6-7 reads, "Do not be anxious about anything, but in everything, by prayer and petition, with thanksgiving, present your requests to God. And the peace of God, which transcends all understanding, will guard your hearts and your minds in Christ Jesus." The Lord gives His people peace. John complements this thought in his second epistle verse three, "Grace, mercy and peace from God the Father and from Jesus Christ, the Father's Son, will be with us in truth and love."

The cross of Christ meant the offer of salvation. Jesus offers eternal life *And Then Some*.

CHAPTER THREE - DOWNWARD

GOD TO US

That Would Have Been Enough!

One of my favorite songs is "Dayenu" which is one of the most famous Passover songs. The Hebrew word "dayenu" implies the idea that the action would have been enough in and of itself and that we would have been satisfied not needing anything more. But of course, God did more. He did the *And Then Some* again and again.

Stanza one says that suppose God helped us escape Egypt, but didn't punish the Egyptian people. That would have been enough. We would have been satisfied.

Stanzas two through five tell that not only did God rescue Israel, but He also punished the Egyptians, destroyed their idols, killed their first-born males, let Israel take the Egyptians' possessions, and separated the Red Sea. Each stanza closes with the thought that each item in and of itself was enough. They would have been satisfied at each turn, but God gave even more.

The next five stanzas state that not only did God rescue Israel from the Red Sea, but He let them cross on dry land, He drowned the oppressors, He provided for Israel in the wilderness, and He fed them manna. God is so good. He constantly went one more step.

The closing stanzas refer to God giving the Sabbath, leading to Mt. Sinai, giving the Torah (the Law), leading Israel to the Promised Land, and building the Temple. Again, each stanza closes with the thought that each item in and of itself was enough. They would have been satisfied, but God gave even more. That Would Have Been Enough!

CHAPTER FOUR - UPWARD

US TO GOD

"The people are bringing more than
enough for doing the work the LORD
commanded to be done"
(Exodus 36:5).

Moses heads up the construction of the sanctuary in Exodus chapter 36. God has chosen Bezalel, Oholiab and every skilled person to do the actual work on the sanctuary. God has gifted them and now gives them the opportunity to express their talent. All of Israel was invited to contribute offerings for the tabernacle. Verse five says the people brought more than enough for doing the work.

After understanding how God has gone way over of what could be expected in His relationship to us, it is only natural to respond back in like manner – *And Then Some*.

There are at least six areas in which we should evaluate our expression of love and gratitude to the Lord.

1. Giving

When it comes to the topic of giving, people typically state something about ten percent and then don't really want to talk about it. Most likely they don't even know where the ten percent principle began and if it truly applies for today.

In Genesis chapter 14 Abram (later renamed Abraham) sets the tone. His nephew, Lot, was kidnapped along with all of Lot's family, neighbors, and possessions. Abram went and recovered Lot, the people and the possessions. Verses eighteen through twenty then bring in the ten-percent principle: "Then Melchizedek king of Salem brought out bread and wine. He was priest of God Most High, and he blessed Abram, saying, 'Blessed be Abram by God Most High, Creator of heaven and earth. And blessed be God Most High, who delivered your enemies into your hand.' Then Abram gave him a tenth of everything." It appears this was a natural response by Abram. Giving a tenth must have been set earlier, but it is not recorded. Hence, the principle continues through Scripture. Jacob commits to give the Lord a tenth of everything in Genesis 28:22, "this stone that I have set up as a pillar will be God's house, and of all that you give me I will give you a tenth."

The giving of possessions continues in Leviticus, "A tithe of everything from the land, whether grain from the soil or fruit from the trees, belongs to the LORD; it is holy to the LORD" (27:30). Leviticus 27:32 extends the ten percent tithe concept, "The entire tithe of the herd and flock—every tenth animal that passes under the shepherd's rod—will be holy to the LORD." Deuteronomy 14:22-23 also is clear on tithing: "Be sure to set aside a tenth of all that your fields produce each year. Eat the tithe of your grain, new wine and oil, and the firstborn of your herds and flocks in the presence of the LORD your God at the place he will choose as a dwelling for his Name, so that you may learn to revere the LORD your God always."

The New Testament continues this thought pattern as the Pharisee prays in Luke 18:12, "I fast twice a week and give a tenth of all I get." Hebrews 7:5 gives a summary, "Now the law requires the descendants of Levi who become priests to collect a tenth from the people—that is, their brothers—even though their brothers are descended from Abraham." From these passages, it would appear that ten percent is the accepted amount. However, we should always consider *And Then Some*. A fuller look at Scripture may convey a more gracious mindset.

"In addition to what you vow and your freewill offerings, prepare these for the LORD at your appointed feasts: your burnt offerings, grain offerings, drink offerings and fellowship offerings" (Numbers 29:39). Throughout the Old Testament it is simply stated as tithes and offerings. Somehow we only kept the idea of a tithe. Nowhere is it recorded to stop the extra giving. Actually, Merrill Unger recorded that Old Testament giving equaled about 23% a year. Not 10%, but 23%! Ten percent went to the priests and Levites; ten percent for the feasts, and every third year ten percent went to the poor. That equaled 23% giving to the Lord. R. K. Hudnut has said, "If every church member were suddenly placed on public relief and gave a tithe of his average welfare payment, the income of American churches would be 35 percent greater." Ten percent may be a notable increase, but God seeks more. He appreciates tithes and offerings. Leviticus chapter seven talks about the fellowship Offering. It was designed for the person who just wanted to say "thank you" to the Lord. It was given out of the goodness of one's heart. It was categorized as strictly a voluntary offering. It was to be given willingly and cheerfully.

It doesn't appear that there is a clear set percent to give. People and churches often become overly concerned with amount. God critiques motive and reasons for giving.

Paul points out in 2 Corinthians 9:7, "Each man should give what he has decided in his heart to give, not reluctantly or under compulsion, for God loves a cheerful giver." A church bulletin recorded, "God loves a cheerful giver. He also accepteth from a grouch." Finances are helpful in reaching the world with the gospel while still training and equipping believers for service. Our support is important, but God wants our positive attitude, not just a few bucks. Financial and emotional support blends together.

Billy Graham did not avoid the topic of tithing in his preaching. He said, "One of the greatest sins in America today is the fact that we are robbing God of that which rightfully belongs to Him. When we don't tithe, we shirk a just debt. Actually we are not giving when we give God one-tenth, for it belongs to Him already. (Leviticus 27:30). This is a debt we owe. Not until we have given a tenth do we actually begin making an offering to the Lord!" Billy Graham could have referenced Malachi 3:8-10, "Will a man rob God? Yet you rob me. 'But you ask, 'How do we rob you?' 'In tithes and offerings. You are under a curse—the whole nation of you—because you are robbing me. Bring the whole tithe into the storehouse, that there may be food in my house. Test me in this,' says the LORD Almighty, 'and see if I will not throw open the floodgates of heaven and pour out so much blessing that you will not have room enough for it.'" To ignore tithing is to rob God. It is scary. Matthew 10:8 reminds, "Freely you have received, freely give." Giving can and should be exciting. It is a privilege to be allowed to assist in the Lord's work. Paul writes in 2 Corinthians 8:3-4, "For I testify that they gave as much as they were able, and even beyond their ability. Entirely on their own, they urgently pleaded with us for the privilege of sharing in this service to the saints." The Macedonian churches even gave beyond their ability. They didn't give out of their excess. They reached deep within their pockets and hearts and gave freely and even beyond their ability. They gave *And Then Some*.

Giving shouldn't be just a topic about money. Acts 3:6 gives a valuable perspective: "Then Peter said, 'Silver or gold I do not have, but what I have I give you. In the name of Jesus Christ of Nazareth, walk.'" There are other ways to be a giving person that has nothing to do with money. We can give our time, attention, gratitude, service, forgiveness and encouragement. Christians should be known by their love which is often expressed through giving of one's self. Billy Graham has also said, "God has given us two hands – one to receive with and the other to give with. We are not cisterns made for hoarding; we are channels made for sharing." To give should be a natural response.

Giving to the Lord isn't a ten percent bargain that relieves guilt. It is about tithes, offerings and sacrifices. It is interesting to think through the thought of sacrifices. When it comes to giving, we should strive "to make a sacrifice" for the Lord. It is not giving until it hurts. It is giving until it feels good. Vance Havner said, "Self, service, substance is the Divine order and nothing counts until we give ourselves." That is giving *And Then Some*.

2. Church Attendance / Involvement

Church attendance is very important. E. C. McKenzie writes, "An empty tomb proves Christianity; an empty church denies it." To say Jesus is Lord and then not attend church is nonsensical. Adults are more creative in excuses for not going to church than students are for not having their homework. Wayne Rice shows how skipping church regularly sounds ridiculous once we relate the usual excuses for not attending church to eating. "I don't eat any more because...

1.   I was forced to eat as a child.

2.   People who eat all the time are hypocrites; they aren't really hungry.

3.   There are so many different kinds of food, I can't decide what to eat.

4.   I used to eat, but I got bored and stopped.

5.   I only eat on special occasions, like Christmas and Easter.

6.   None of my friends will eat with me.

7.   I'll start eating when I get older.

8.   I really don't have time to eat.

9.   I don't believe that eating does anybody any good. It's just a crutch.

10.   Restaurants and grocery stores are only after your money."

There really should be more effort in getting involved in a local church than in creating excuses to serve oneself. Church attendance and involvement is not an option. The whole issue needs to be Christ focused, not self promotion. Vance Havner challenges another excuse when he said, "We are hearing today about those who like Christ but do not like the church. But Christ loved the church and gave Himself for it. How can we like the Head, but not the Body, the Groom, but not the Bride?" Having realized all that Christ has done and will do, compels one to be involved. Christ died for us, rose again, and is coming back. We need to see where we can relate and help. As Paul Lee Tan has noted, a Christian not being involved in a church is like:

- A student who will not go to school.
- A soldier who will not join an army.
- A citizen who does not pay taxes or vote.
- A salesman with no customers.
- An explorer with no base camp.
- A seaman on a ship without a crew.
- A businessman on a deserted island.
- An author without readers.
- A tuba player without an orchestra.
- A parent without a family.
- A football player without a team.
- A politician who is a hermit.
- A scientist who does not share his findings.
- A bee without a hive.

It is illogical to assume one can be a Christian and not attend church regularly. It has to be unnatural. Moody Monthly gave a clever comparison for those who just want to stay home and listen to a sermon, "The difference between listening to a radio sermon and going to church...is almost like the difference between calling your girl on the phone and spending an evening with her." Obviously there is nothing like being there.

It is good to become a little introspective concerning church attendance. It is good to ask, "Why do I go to church?

Do I go to get or give?" Hopefully, it is a mixture of getting and giving. A common Sunday afternoon question is, "How was church?" All too often, the answer is centered on the sermon. We evaluate how encouraging or convicting the message was for us. James Kennedy said, "Most people think of the church as a drama, with the minister as the chief actor, God as the prompter, and the laity as the critic. What is actually the case is that the congregation is the chief actor, the minister is the prompter, and God is the critic."

Hebrews 10:25 gives a forgotten reason for church attendance, " Let us not give up meeting together, as some are in the habit of doing, but let us encourage one another—and all the more as you see the Day approaching." It should first be noted that missing church is habit forming. We need to be careful because before we know it we are committing to other activities like sleeping, reading, exercising, or encountering nature. Hunting, golfing, fishing and boating may bring one into God's presence through natural revelation. Yet, there is more to church than just being in God's presence. Bad habits need to be broken. The other point to observe from Hebrews refers to the purpose of going to church. It is not just to come into God's presence. It is to encourage one another. This verse makes it clear that we should go to church to also give. It would be refreshing to hear people answer the "how was church question" with answers centered around encouragement. We should approach church with the mindset of looking for opportunities to encourage others. We will also see that when we need encouragement, it will be returned to us.

David has the ideal attitude in Psalm 122:1, "I rejoiced with those who said to me, 'Let us go to the house of the LORD.'" Sunday should be such an exciting day. Worship was changed to Sunday to celebrate the Lord's resurrection. He is alive! Since He is alive, we have hope and a future. It is exciting to be a child of God. Vance Havner again said, "The church has no greater need today than to fall in love with Jesus all over again." We need to remember all that Jesus has done for us. He went over and above the call of duty to relate to us. He understands. He wants and expects our love. E. C. McKenzie wrote, "The surest steps toward happiness are the church steps." We can't afford to miss church. We have too much to give and can also gain a lot from others.

Vance Havner admonishes, "Don't ever come to church without coming as though it were the first time, as though it could be the best time and as though it might be the last time." It is good to come to church with a fresh mind and heart anticipating something special to happen. It is going to church with the idea that God is about to surprise us from

His Word or through someone's actions. I need to make the most of this opportunity. Rumanian Law No. 153/190 Article 1-D appears humorous. It banned Rumanian citizens from "coming together to play cards, drink alcohol, or waste time." What is not as funny is the fact that numbers of Christians were being arrested, fined, and even imprisoned for going to church and "wasting time." It is understood that communist authorities would view Christian activity as 'wasting time.' However, how do we view church? The challenge is to make sure that we don't waste time. We need to make the most of every opportunity because the days are evil. We need to encourage others and press on.

3. Evangelism

Evangelism is not the art of forcing Christ on others. It is not a drive-by verse launching. Evangelism is the sharing of one's self. Being transparent with beliefs, thoughts, and life are important. It largely involves witnessing through a consistent lifestyle. It is not just about 'talk,' but it includes our 'walk.' We need to walk the talk and talk the walk.

It should be obvious that we need to tell others about Jesus. In what has come to be called the Great Commission, Jesus said, "Therefore go and make disciples of all nations, baptizing them in the name of the Father and of the Son and of the

Holy Spirit, and teaching them to obey everything I have commanded you. And surely I am with you always, to the very end of the age" (Matthew 28:19-20). Emphasis is also placed on 'going' in Mark 16:15, "Go into all the world and preach the good news to all creation." Telling others about Jesus is definitely our responsibility.

Romans 10:13-14 can sound a little sarcastic, "'Everyone who calls on the name of the Lord will be saved.' How, then, can they call on the one they have not believed in? And how can they believe in the one of whom they have not heard? And how can they hear without someone preaching to them?" It almost implies that early Christians were wondering if they needed to witness. Paul gently roars that if we don't speak, they can't hear, if they can't hear, then they can't believe, and if they don't believe, then they will be lost forever. Christians must go and preach the good news of Jesus Christ.

Paul clearly proclaimed in 2 Corinthians 4:5, "For we do not preach ourselves, but Jesus Christ as Lord, and ourselves as your servants for Jesus' sake." Christians need to go out and talk. But the talk shouldn't only be about them, we need to talk about Jesus. It appears everyone loves to talk about themselves, yet we must refrain and focus on Jesus. Everyone needs to know of God's love. The God who created us wants to have a relationship with us. But our sin blocked the path to God. A huge gap was left. The gap could only be covered by the cross of Jesus Christ. Yes, Jesus died for our sins, He was buried, and He rose again. Now He is alive, and offers us life: eternal and abundant. It is exciting to be involved in God's work of giving new life.

When my son was young, he asked, "Dad, why don't we go straight to Heaven as soon as we accept Christ as Savior?" His question was sincere and actually quite deep. Obviously, we need to stay on earth to tell others about Jesus. If Christians immediately went to Heaven, who would have been around to tell us the good news of salvation?

Our witnessing needs to include preaching, but not only preaching. It is important to live the life. Evangelism includes preaching *And Then Some*. Vance Havner made a terrifying observation. He said, "There is not much connection between what most of us do at church on Sunday, and the way we live the rest of the week." Referring to the gospel, he added, "If it cannot be lived in the shop, there is no sense in preaching it in the sanctuary." We need to realize that our lives are a manifestation of what we think about God. Our actions are a reflection of what we truly believe. What we say is meaningless if we don't act consistently with our own message.

Paul's prayer life for his friends focused on consistent living, "And we pray this in order that you may live a life worthy of the Lord and may please him in every way: bearing fruit in every good work, growing in the knowledge of God" (Colossians 1:10). Living a life worthy of the Lord is extreme, but it is crucial in order to be taken seriously.

The philosopher Soren Kierkegaard shared an illustration about a circus that caught fire. The flames from the circus were getting out of control and started to spread to the fields around the circus grounds. Soon the fire was headed toward the nearby village. The circus master was convinced that the village people would be killed by the fire. He asked for someone to go to the village and warn the people of the coming fire. A clown, dressed in full makeup and costume, jumped on a bike and rode down to the village to warn the people. The clown rode up and down the streets yelling, "Run for your lives! Run for your lives! A fire is coming and the village is going to burn! The village is going to burn! Run for your lives!" The village people came out of their shops and homes when they heard the clown. They shouted, laughed and applauded the clown. They enjoyed his performance. The harder he tried to convince them, the more they laughed. The village did burn and numerous people died. They would have been saved if they would have listened to the clown. However, he was just a clown. Soren's illustration is very challenging. If we just clown around and don't practice what we preach, people will not take us or Jesus seriously. Miguel de Cervantes wrote, "He who lives well is the best preacher." It is important to remember that the only Bible some people will read is our lives.

A beautiful account is recorded in Acts 4:13: "When they saw the courage of Peter and John and realized that they were unschooled, ordinary men, they were astonished and they took note that these men had been with Jesus." The people not only heard the message, they also "saw" it. Often actions speak louder than words. The people saw something different and wanted to know more. When we spend time with Jesus and truly get to know Him, it will be evident to others because of changed lives. People will give the excuse that they don't witness because they don't know what to say. This passage encourages us to realize that unschooled, ordinary people can reflect Jesus and be a valuable witness.

The difference between the ordinary Christian and an extraordinary Christian can be summarized in just three words: *And Then Some*. To be extra for God is to live extra every day and in every place. J. Wilbur Chapman lived the extra-ordinary life, "The rule that governs my life is this: Anything that dims my vision of Christ, or takes away my taste for Bible study, or cramps my prayer life, or makes Christian work difficult, is wrong for me, and I must, as a Christian, turn away from it." This same commitment to daily living was expressed by John Donne, "I count all that part of my life lost which I spent not in communion with God, or in doing good." This is the mindset that Paul expressed in Philippians 1:21, "For to me, to live is Christ and to die is gain." My life belongs to Him.

Philosophy students love to go back to the sayings of Socrates. However, Christianity is more than just philosophy. It is more than just ideas to be scrutinized. It involves our lives. Socrates understood this in his statement, "The end of life is to be like God, and the soul following God will be like him." To follow Christ means to live like Him. To be Christian means to be Christ like. Hudson Taylor explained the Christian walk in a more practical way, "If your father and mother, your sister and brother, if the very cat and dog in the house, are not happier for your being Christian, it is a question whether you really are one."

Paul sets the ultimate personal challenge when he says," Follow my example, as I follow the example of Christ" (1 Corinthians 11:1). We need to live at such a level that we set an example that others can follow. It is not just do what I say, but do as I do. It is not a well-worded lecture, it is hands-on learning.

It is good to end each day with an overview of the day. One should ask what he did that day that no one but a Christian would have done. He should also recognize things he did because he was a Christian. Finally, it is good to review things that as a Christian he shouldn't have done, and make plans to correct the situation.

A telling story is told of Saint Francis of Assisi. He told several of his followers, "Let us go to the village over the way and preach." As they went on their way, they met a man who was feeling low. Francis was in no hurry, and he stopped to listen and encourage the man. He then went to the village. In the village he spent time with the people. Francis talked with shopkeepers, spent time with the farmers at their fruit and vegetable stands, and played with the children in the streets. On the way back home, they met a farmer with a load of hay. Francis spent time with him. Finally, with the morning gone, they were back at the monastery. One of Francis' followers was disappointed with the morning trip. He said, "Brother Francis, you said you were going to preach. The morning is spent and no sermon has been given." Saint Francis responded, "But we have been preaching all the way." It is how we live every moment that witnesses for or against Christ.

A quote I have framed in my office summarizes this whole section. It is St. Francis of Assisi's famous statement, "Preach the Gospel at all times...if necessary, use words."

4. The Word
Read it

Someone has said, "It's a terrible responsibility to own a Bible." The best-selling book of all time should not be solely a decorative piece. It must be read. It should be noted: "The three greatest sins of today are indifference to, neglect of, and disrespect for the Word of God." This makes too much sense. People love but ignore their Bible. L. R.

Akers captures an all too-true point when he said, "There are ten men who will fight for the Bible to one who will read it." We brag about the Bible, but don't read it. We spend quite a bit of money on a leather edition with fancy print, but don't read it. We are troubled that we can not carry it into public schools, but we don't read it. We will fight for it, but not read it?

David F. Nygren expresses some exaggeration in sarcasm when he said, "If all the neglected Bibles were dusted simultaneously, we would have a record dust storm and the sun would go into eclipse for a whole week." All humor aside, this is a sad commentary on the Christian world. We own numerous Bibles and will fight over a certain translation, but do we read it?

The King James Version, New King James Version, New American Standard Bible, New International Version, New Living Translation, Contemporary English Version, The Message, The Living Bible, The Amplified Bible, English Standard Version – which is best? It really doesn't matter if we don't read it!

I have visited several churches recently. One common observation is that more people bring their cell phones to church than their Bibles. I believe most church members would be more inclined to hurry home and get a forgotten cell phone than a misplaced Bible. This shouldn't be so.

I realize this isn't true of everyone. John Quincy Adams said, "I have for many years made it a practice to read through the Bible once a year. My custom is to read four or five chapters every morning immediately after rising from my bed. It employs about an hour of my time, and seems to me the most suitable manner of beginning the day. In what light soever we regard the Bible, whether with reference to revelation, to history, or to morality, it is an invaluable and inexhaustible mine of knowledge and virtue." Douglas MacArthur also had the same diligence, "Believe me, sir, never a night goes by, be I ever so tired, but I read the Word of God before I go to bed."

As Christians we should have read through the whole Bible. It doesn't take that long. Eleanor Doan has figured out that it takes 70 hours and 40 minutes to read the Bible at pulpit rate. Obviously, we could read it faster silently. Presently, I just finished going through the book of Leviticus again. I realize some might wonder why anyone would spend time in the Old Testament. However, all sixty-six books are God's Word. We should read the 'whole' Bible. Leviticus has renewed my strength. It is so refreshing to realize that kosher eating sounds like a present day Dietary Manual – avoid red meat, shell fish, pork, and meat fat. Moses wrote this some 3,400 years ago. Reading Leviticus has reminded me to voluntarily give offerings to the Lord. God's people are to be unique, set apart for something special. God's Word is so special. I feel like Ezekiel when he wrote, "Then he said to me, 'Son of man, eat this scroll I am giving you and fill your stomach with it.' So I ate it, and it tasted as sweet as honey in my mouth" (Ezekiel 3:3).

Paul Lee Tan noted, "Warning: This book is habit-forming. Regular use causes loss of anxiety, decreased appetite for lying, cheating, stealing, hating. Symptoms: increased sensations of love, peace, joy, compassion." Reading the Word changes us and hence the world around us. The Word of God is alive.

Learn it

It is not enough to just read the Bible. A. Morgan Derham points out, "The Bible is not like a slot machine. If you put in five minutes' reading time, you don't necessarily get a 'blessing' (or anything else) out of it." Unfortunately, there appears to be an unspoken rule that God immediately owes us one if we read for five minutes. It is not talked about, but the slot machine analogy seems prevalent.

Scripture is clear that the Bible needs to be read and studied. Paul sets the challenge in 2 Timothy 2:15 where he writes, "Do your best to present yourself to God as one approved, a workman who does not need to be ashamed and who correctly handles the word of truth." Studying the Scripture prepares one for the present and future. It is important to understand God's Word so we can use it effectively to encourage and challenge ourselves and others.

Ezra's reputation was put in print. Ezra 7:10 says, "For Ezra had devoted himself to the study and observance of the Law of the LORD, and to teaching its decrees and laws in Israel." What a testimony to be known as one who devotes himself to studying God's Word. Ezra not only studied it, but he obeyed God's commands. Bible reading and studying should be part of the Christian's daily routine.

One final thought: We should study the Bible as a privilege, not as a duty. It is such a blessing to own a copy of God's Word in our language. It is not reading because one has to, but because one is allowed to.

Memorize and Meditate

Wayne Rice encourages us to imagine: Jesus takes His disciples up the mountain and teaches Matthew 5:3-10 for the first time, "Blessed are the poor in spirit, for theirs is the kingdom of heaven. Blessed are those who mourn, for they will be comforted. Blessed are the meek, for they will inherit the earth. Blessed are those who hunger and thirst for righteousness, for they will be filled. Blessed are the merciful, for they will be shown mercy. Blessed are the pure in heart, for they will see God. Blessed are the peacemakers, for they will be called sons of God. Blessed are those who are persecuted because of righteousness, for theirs is the kingdom of heaven."

> *Simon Peter asks*, "Do we have to write this down?"
>
> *Andrew adds,* "Are we going to have a test on this?"
>
> *Philip complains,* "I don't have any paper."
>
> *Bartholomew asked,* "Do we have to turn this in?"
>
> *John whined,* "The other disciples didn't have to learn this."
>
> *Matthew requested,* "May I go to the bathroom?"
>
> *Judas pleaded,* "Will we get paid for this?"
>
> *James said,* "I don't get it!"

Then one of the Pharisees who was present asked Jesus for His lesson plan and inquired of Him, "Where are your theological imperatives and long-term objectives in the cognitive domain?"

And Jesus wept.

As a teacher, I understand this illustration all too well. Laziness is common place. When it comes to God's

Word, there should be no question that it is to be studied, including memorization and meditation. God preserved His Word all these years and is making it available in numerous languages. Therefore, it makes sense to memorize verses and sections of the Bible. Meditation then is made possible as one formulates thought patterns based on God's Word.

Prosperity and success only appear in Scripture when meditation of the Word is stated. Joshua 1:8 says, "Do not let this Book of the Law depart from your mouth; meditate on it day and night, so that you may be careful to do everything written in it. Then you will be prosperous and successful." Meditation becomes a habit that takes place as one drives, walks, shops, and carries on through the day.

Psalm 1:1-2 doesn't speak of prosperity and success, but God's blessing is given, "Blessed is the man who does not walk in the counsel of the wicked or stand in the way of sinners or sit in the seat of mockers. But his delight is in the law of the LORD, and on his law he meditates day and night." Meditating on God's Word regularly leads to a blessed life. Gipsy Smith summarizes this mindset well, "What makes the difference is not how many times you have been through the Bible, but how many times and how thoroughly the Bible has been through you."

Let it sink in deeper

"In a day of tranquilizers we are likely to make an aspirin pill of religion. The Word of God is not a lullaby to put us to sleep but a reveille to wake us up." Vance Havner really captures the essence of Christianity for too many. The world sees a weak, inconsistent Christianity and they often refer to it as a crutch. Christianity is not about me. It is not to be selfish. It is a wake-up call to growth.

Reading the Bible should lead to strong study habits. This study should lead to memorization and meditation. The next step is to let the Bible sink in and change our lives. Psalm 119:11 says, "I have hidden your word in my heart that I might not sin against you." Once God's Word takes a hold of us, it should affect our thoughts and actions. Dwight

L. Moody had a creative way of summarizing the meaning of this verse, "Sin will keep you from this Book. This Book will keep you from sin." It is true that laziness, poor planning, and lack of initiative keep one from exploring through the Bible. It is also true that knowing the Word and its Author changes lives forever. Vance Havner hits it on the head, "If you see a Bible that is falling apart, it probably belongs to someone who isn't!"

Again, reading, studying, memorization and meditation of Scripture are so important, but it is the *And Then Some* of letting God take over through His Word that changes everything. This is adversely demonstrated through the life and death of the prince of Grenada.

Wayne Rice tells the story of the prince of Grenada, an heir to the Spanish crown, who was thrown in prison. It was Madrid's dreadful prison called "The Place of the Skull." The prince was given only one book to read. He was given the Bible. Since it was all he had to read, he read it from cover to cover numerous times. He was known to always have it with him. Finally, after thirty-three years of imprisonment, he died. In cleaning out his cell, they found several notes on the walls. The prince had used nails to carve notes into the soft stone prison walls. His notes contained some detailed observations:

Psalm 118:8 is the middle verse of the Bible,

Ezra 7:21 contains all the letters of the alphabet except the letter j,

Esther 8:9 is the longest verse in the Bible,

No word or name in the Bible has more than six syllables.

From all that is known, the prince never gave his life to Christ. It is horrible to realize that a man can study the Word of God for thirty-three years and only come away with trivia.

William A. Ward summarizes this section in a quick quote, "It is not enough to own a Bible; we must read it. It is not enough to read it; we must let it speak to us. It is not enough to let it speak to us; we must believe it. It is not enough to believe it; we must live it." Another way of viewing the *And Then Some* of Scripture is to go to your Bible regularly, open it prayerfully, read it expectantly, live it joyfully.

5. Prayer

J. Edgar Hoover said, "The spectacle of a nation praying is more awe-inspiring than the explosion of an atomic bomb. The force of prayer is greater than any possible combination of man-controlled powers, because prayer is man's greatest means of trapping the infinite resources of God." That is a powerful quote. I personally believe we 'tap' not 'trap' the infinite resources of God. However, I still think the quote is valuable. Most Christians would enjoy the quote, agree with the quote, hit out a hearty "Amen," and then continue to pray prayers that if they were dynamite, we wouldn't have enough to blow our noses.

The question of when to pray has several answers.

Daily morning: People tend to have a morning routine. From alarm clock, shaving, shower, getting dressed, grabbing breakfast and maybe even a little update from the newspaper, there are some definite steps taken each morning. King David states in Psalm 5:3 that part of his schedule included prayer, "In the morning, O LORD, you hear my voice; in the morning I lay my requests before you and wait in expectation." Each morning David would pray and listen. The sons of Korah also set time each morning. They wrote in Psalm 88:13, "But I cry to you for help, O LORD; in the morning my prayer comes before you." It is important to start the day with prayer.

Robert A. Cook said, "Pray your way through the day. You can't see around the turning of life's corners, but God can. When the alarm goes off, instead of saying, 'Good lord – morning!' say, 'Good morning, Lord!'" Instead of dreading what the day may hold, we should look with excitement how God may use us to make a difference this very day. My favorite morning prayer comes from Norman Grubb, "Good morning, God, I love You! What are You up to today? I want to be part of it." I want to have the mindset that God leads me through the day. I try to avoid the prayer work list that tells God what I am doing and invites Him to tag along. I don't want God to be my co-pilot. I want to be His personal assistant.

John Bunyan pointed out that, "He who runs from God in the morning will scarcely find Him the rest of the day." Paul Lee Tan uses poetry to show it is dangerous to start the day running alone.

> I got up early one morning and rushed into the day;
>
> I had so much to accomplish I didn't have time to pray.
>
> Troubles just tumbled about me and heavier came each task;
>
> Why doesn't God help me, I wondered, He answered, "You didn't ask."
>
> I tried to come into God's presence, I used all the keys at the lock.
>
> God gently and lovingly chided, "My child, you didn't knock."
>
> I wanted to see joy and beauty, but the day

toiled on grey and bleak,

I called on the Lord for the reason – He said, "You didn't seek."

I woke up early this morning and paused before entering the day.

I had so much to accomplish that I had to take time to pray.

A cute story is told about a little girl who each night threw one shoe under her bed before going to sleep. Her mother was curious as to why. The little girl said, "My teacher says that if we have to kneel by our beds to look for our shoes, we'll remember to keep kneeling and say our morning prayers." That is more than just another cute story by Paul Lee Tan, it is good advice. Drop a shoe. Drop a knee. Start the day with prayer.

Twice a day: Starting each day with prayer is important, but it only makes sense to end the day the same way. Psalm 88:1 says, "O LORD, the God who saves me, day and night I cry out before you." George Herbert paints an accurate picture, "Prayer should be the key of the day and the lock of the night." Prayer opens the day and secures our night into God's hands. It has been said, "Hem in both ends of the day with prayer, and then it won't be so likely to unravel in the middle." The point is plain and simple. When we take time with God, He takes time for us.

Three times a day: When people think of praying three times a day they tend to relate it to meals. They answer that they pray three times a day, right before each meal. It is commendable to pray before meals expressing gratitude to God for supplying our needs; however, Psalm 55:17 stresses prayer three times a day just to converse with God, "Evening, morning and noon I cry out in distress, and he hears my voice."

A favorite Bible story involves Daniel in the lion's den. Remember that Daniel was thrown to the lions because he prayed openly three times a day. Daniel 6:10 records, "Now when Daniel learned that the decree had been published, he went home to his upstairs room where the windows opened toward Jerusalem. Three times a day he got down on his knees and prayed, giving thanks to his God, just as he had done before." Daniel was being watched, hunted and even trapped, yet his prayer is a prayer of thanksgiving. He didn't take a wish list to God three times a day. He conversed with God recognizing His involvement in man's daily walk.

All night: The next time element for prayer is the example of Jesus Himself. Luke 6:12 is so profound, "One of those days Jesus went out to a mountainside to pray, and spent the night praying to God." Jesus, who is God, felt He needed to pray all night. If Jesus needed to pray, then we definitely need extended periods of prayer. It is interesting that people can

77

talk on the phone or sit at the computer emailing for hours, but find five minute prayers to be too long. How many minutes is the average cell phone contract? Does that include unlimited nights and weekends? It is easy to live with a phone to the ear constantly. It shows the importance of relationships and connecting with others. We need to do the same with God.

Without stopping: Finally, after examining how we should pray every morning, morning and night, three times a day, and all night, Paul hits us with a lifestyle of prayer. 1 Thessalonians 5:16-18 gives God's will, or desire, for Christians, "Be joyful always; pray continually; give thanks in all circumstances, for this is God's will for you in Christ Jesus." God's desire is joy, prayer, and thankfulness. God wants us to pray constantly. It is the attitude of walking through life connected to Him. Walter A. Mueller expressed this same sentiment, "Prayer is not merely an occasional impulse to which we respond when we are in trouble: prayer is a life attitude."

A common complaint of prayer is that it doesn't feel like anyone is listening. Prayer seems like talking to the air or a machine. Most people get frustrated with answering machines or calling a company and talking to an automated service instead of a person. Also, all too often when we need something, the company is in a different time zone or it is just after hours. A humorous phone message by Wayne Rice is attributed to a Psychiatric Hot Line, "Welcome to the Psychiatric Hot Line.

- If you are obsessive-compulsive, repeatedly press 1.
- If you are codependent, ask someone to press 2.
- If you have multiple personalities, press 3, 4, and 5.
- If you are suffering from paranoia, we know who you are and what you want. Stay on the line until we trace the call.
- If you are schizophrenic, listen carefully and a little voice will tell you which number to press.
- If you are bipolar, it doesn't matter which number you press. No one will answer.
- If you are depressed, push any button you wish. It won't make any difference anyhow.

Thank you for your call."

Fortunately, we can call God at any time, from any place. We will not be put on hold. We do not have to leave a message hoping someone eventually gets back to us. He is excited and ready for us. He welcomes regular calls. We never have to ask, "Can you hear me now?"

Jesus told a parable of a persistent widow. Jesus' message was about constantly praying. He tells us to pray without ceasing. Luke 18:1 says, "Then Jesus told his

disciples a parable to show them that they should always pray and not give up." Jesus' message was to pray, and when you finish, pray some more.

Prayer: we need more of it

Most Christians would admit that more personal prayer is needed. Developing the consistent habit of regularly going to the Lord is needed. Abraham Lincoln understood this when he said, "I have been driven many times to my knees by the overwhelming conviction that I had nowhere else to go. My own wisdom, and that of all about me, seemed insufficient for the day." There is no better place to go than God Himself.

Abraham Lincoln developed a reputation for being a man of prayer. It is a recommended goal that one becomes known as a person of prayer. In Acts 10:2 Cornelius' resume is abbreviated, "He and all his family were devout and God-fearing; he gave generously to those in need and prayed to God regularly." Cornelius was known for praying to God regularly. David too, had this reputation. In Psalm 109:4 David talks about people treating him poorly, but he is okay because, "In return for my friendship they accuse me, but I am a man of prayer." David takes comfort and even a little pride in the statement that he is a man of prayer.

Paul Lee Tan recorded that John Wesley spent at least two hours each day in prayer. Samuel Rutherford rose at three o'clock each morning to wait upon God. Martin Luther set apart his three best hours for prayer. Luther said, "I have so much to do, that I cannot get on without three hours a day praying." It is safe to say that Wesley, Rutherford, and Luther were men of prayer.

The story is told by Wayne Rice of a young man looking for a job. He went to a logging foreman and asked for a job. The foreman had him cut down a tree to see his skills. The young man did a quick, efficient job and was hired immediately. Monday, Tuesday, and Wednesday went great, but Thursday was different. The foreman came to the young man and told him to pick up his check on his way out. The young man asked why he was fired. The foreman explained that the young man went from being one of the best loggers on Monday to being the slowest logger on Thursday. The young man objected stating that he was a hard worker, arriving first, leaving last and working through most breaks. The foreman couldn't explain the decline until he asked, "Have you been sharpening your axe?" The young man replied that he had been working too hard and didn't have time to sharpen his axe. The analogy is obvious. Work and schedule are so hectic there appears to be no time for prayer. However, prayer is essential to stay sharp.

Paul commanded in Colossians 4:2, "Devote yourselves to prayer, being watchful and thankful." We need to be individuals devoted to prayer. Prayer needs to be a priority. We need to increase the amount of time spent with God.

Samuel gives a challenging twist. In his farewell speech to Israel, he said, "As for me, far be it from me that I should sin against the LORD by failing to pray for you. And I will teach you the way that is good and right" (1 Samuel 12:23). Not praying is a sin. Prayer is helpful and mandatory.

Be Sincere

Spending more time in prayer is important, but we need to be sincere. John Bunyan said, "In prayer it is better to have a heart without words than words without a heart." God knows our hearts. He truly sees right through us, and we are transparent before Him. In Scripture, we have some beautiful examples of sincere prayer:

"Hannah was praying in her heart, and her lips were moving but her voice was not heard. Eli thought she was drunk" (1 Samuel 1:13). Hannah was so sincere in her prayer that she didn't realize her physical response. She didn't care. She was focused and real before God.

The same scenario is seen in Jesus. Luke 22:44 says, "And being in anguish, he prayed more earnestly, and his sweat was like drops of blood falling to the ground." Jesus so physically devoted Himself to prayer that it became a major workout. He put everything into prayer. He didn't just go through the motions; neither did He quote repetitious phrases in a 'holy tone.' He sincerely poured out His spirit before and to God the Father.

Finally, there is the example of the Holy Spirit. Vance Havner summarizes it better than anyone, "The Holy Spirit prays for us with unutterable groanings. If He groans for us, we might well agonize in prayer for ourselves!" So, according to these examples, we need to regularly and sincerely pour out our hearts to the Lord.

We need to pray and work

Pope Xystus I said, "God does not listen to the prayer of the lazy." Prayer needs to be accompanied by action. Proverbs 15:8 says, "The LORD detests the sacrifice of the wicked, but the prayer of the upright pleases him." The difference between the wicked and the upright would definitely be motive, but Solomon would have also noticed the difference in their actions. Jeremiah had the mindset of a mature believer. He said in chapter forty-two and verse three, "Pray that the LORD your God will tell us where we should go and what we should do." Going and doing require action. Jeremiah tells us to pray and act. Don't be lazy and then blame God for your shortcomings.

St. Augustine too, gives some practical theology, "Pray as though everything depended on God. Work as though everything depended on you." Similar advice is stated in a couple of cultural proverbs. A German Proverb advises, "Pray as though no work would help, and work as though no prayer would help." Similarly a Russian Proverb reminds, "Pray to God, but row for the shore."

The picture that I like best is that God doesn't steer a parked car. We need to pray and then start moving. God directs when we move. God wants to work through us, not in spite of us.

Finally, Phillips Brooks gives clear direction, "O, do not pray for easy lives. Pray to be stronger men. Do not pray for tasks equal to your powers. Pray for powers equal to your tasks." We need to pray often. Our prayers need to be sincere. We need to add feet to our prayers. It is exciting to watch God use us in answering our own prayers. Before jumping into action, part of our prayer time should be silently listening for our orders from our Commander-in-chief.

We need to pray and listen

Listening really brings new light to the concept of prayer. Prayer is normally viewed as what to say. Prayer is talk *And Then Some*.

Janet L. Weaver understands this concept, "Be still, and in the quiet moments, listen to the voice of your heavenly Father. His words can renew your spirit. No one knows you and your needs like He does." One of my favorite verses is Psalm 46:10. I need the reminder to, "Be still, and know that I am God."

George Washington Carver said, "My prayers seem to be more of an attitude than anything else. I indulge in no lip service, but ask the great God silently, daily, and often many times a day, to permit me to speak to Him. I ask Him to give me wisdom, understanding and bodily strength to do His will. Hence, I am asking and receiving all the time." Asking and receiving equates speaking and listening.

Clement of Alexandria gives a very elementary definition of prayer, "Prayer is conversation with God." Conversation consists of at least two parties responding back and forth to each other. Prayer is not just a one-sided presentation.

Frank C. Laubach continues the thought, "Prayer at its highest is a two-way conversation – and for me the most important part is listening to God's replies." George Mueller summarizes everything when he said that the most important part of prayer was the fifteen minutes after he had said 'Amen.'

Prayer: Give or get?

An excellent question to ask concerning our Christian activity is, "Is my motive to give or get?" Do we pray to get something from God or to give Him something or both? A helpful acronym for prayer is ACTS: Adoration, Confession, Thanksgiving, and Supplication. This brings a good balance of giving and getting in our interaction with God.

Ralph Waldo Emerson bluntly said, "Prayer that craves a particular commodity, anything less than all good, is vicious... Prayer as a means to a private end is meanness and theft." Prayer should not be selfish in nature. Prayer is more than asking God to run errands for us. However, often the only time we have for prayer focuses on requests. We are too busy to just sit around to chat and listen.

The story is told of an older lady who came to meet with President Abraham Lincoln. She brought a basket into his private office. President Lincoln asked what he could do for her. She replied, "Mr. President, I have come here today not to ask any favor for myself or for anyone. I heard you were very fond of cookies, and I came here to bring you this basket of cookies!" Tears came down his face. After a prolonged moment of silence, he said, "My good woman, your thoughtful and unselfish deed greatly moves me. Thousands have come into this office since I became President, but you are the first one to come asking no favor for yourself or somebody else!" This story should display much of our prayer time. These are moments when we call just to say, "Hi, what are You up to?"

One night a little girl surprised her mother when she concluded her prayer for her family and friends by adding, "And now, God, what can I do for You?" That is beautiful. Often we can learn major lessons from children. We need to respect childlike faith.

Don't expect a thousand-dollar answer to a ten cent prayer.

6. Service

Most people are familiar with Exodus chapter twenty. It contains the Ten Commandments. However, few people look to the next chapter. Exodus 21 addresses the regulations concerning servants. Servants were set free the seventh year. Due to some circumstances, a servant may want to remain a servant for life. Exodus 21:5-6 states, "But if the servant declares, 'I love my master and my wife and children and do not want to go free,' then his master must take him before the judges. He shall take him to the door or

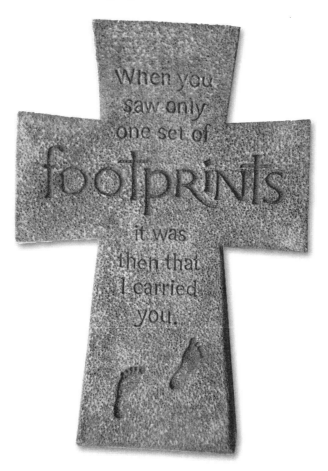

the doorpost and pierce his ear with an awl. Then he will be his servant for life." A pierced ear was a sign that someone had a special master and chose to be his servant for life. I am not encouraging a special piercing, but we do have an awesome Master and should choose to be His servants for life.

David seemed to have a full understanding of fully devoting himself to the Lord. In Psalm 40:6 he writes, "Sacrifice and offering you did not desire, but my ears you have pierced; burnt offerings and sin offerings you did not require." Figuratively speaking, David viewed himself as having his ear pierced for God. He chose to be a servant for life to the Lord. David's service involved more than just making some sacrifices. It consisted of more than going to church on Sunday and maybe one week night. In fact, it means giving God your entire life.

Vance Havner points out, "The average church member would do well to look in his concordance and see how many columns it takes to list all the 'serve,' 'servant,' 'service' references. We come to church to sit but will not go out to serve." Service is crucial and expected for a Christian.

The story is told about a young artist who had painted his version of the Last Supper. When he finished, he asked Tolstoy, the famous Russian writer, for his opinion. Tolstoy pointed to the central figure and said, "You do not love Him." The artist exclaimed, "Why that is the Lord Jesus Christ."

Tolstoy retorted, "I know, but you do not love Him. If you loved Him more, you would paint Him better." Due to our love for the Lord, we should want to serve Him to the best of our ability. If we loved Him, we would serve Him better.

Psalm 2:11 expresses two unique emotions in serving the Lord, "Serve the LORD with fear and rejoice with trembling." Our service expresses reverence for God Almighty while excitement follows to be allowed to be part of His doings. Such service brings joy. The roots of happiness grow deepest in the soil of service.

Deuteronomy 10:12 brings God's request for us, "And now, O Israel, what does the LORD your God ask of you but to fear the LORD your God, to walk in all his ways, to love him, to serve the LORD your God with all your heart and with all your soul." First, this was stated to Israel, but it definitely applies to all of God's children. Second, it should be taken stronger than just a request of God, but applied as a commandment.

Deuteronomy 6:13-14 continues the mindset of service being expected or required of God's children, "Fear the LORD your God, serve him only and take your oaths in his name. Do not follow other gods, the gods of the peoples around you." This section is even quoted in the New Testament. Jesus when being tempted by Satan says, "It is

written: 'Worship the Lord your God and serve him only"
(Luke 4:8). Christians are to serve God with all their being.

God wants to use us in the ministry. Often we make
excuses or limit individuals from their ability to fully serve
the Lord. In the following letter, author Wayne Rice uses
humor to make some points on serving God:

Dear Brothers and Sisters in Christ,

Grace and peace to you from God
our Father and from the Lord Jesus Christ.
Understanding that your pulpit is vacant, I'd
like to be considered for the job. You see,
I love to preach, even though my preaching
tends to stir up quite a bit of controversy.
In fact, one of my sermons caused a riot.
Actually, I've never been able to stay in one
place more than three years.

My health isn't too good. I have
what I call a 'thorn in the flesh – and to be
perfectly honest, I'm not much to look at. I
can assure you, however, that this doesn't
interfere with my ministry. I'm a bachelor
by choice – never been married and never
had any kids – but I'm surprisingly good at
conducting family life seminars.

If you do a background check
on me – and I'm sure you will – you'll
probably discover that I changed my name
a while back, and I have been arrested a few
times. But even in jail I was able to have a

successful ministry. People tell me I'm quite a theologian, although I've never attended seminary.

I hope you aren't looking for an administrator. I'm not too good at keeping records. And my memory's not too good. Sometimes I forget who I've baptized, for instance. But I'm a hard worker, although the things I want to do, I rarely do. And the things I don't want to do, I always end up doing. Go figure. But you know what? I've found that everything works out fine in the end for those who love God and are called according to His purpose. Praise be to God.

Well, let me know if you are interested. I can start next week. By the way, I wrote this with my own hand.

Grace to you all,

Paul

Paul lived an intriguing life. He is viewed as one of the greatest ministers of all time. Yet, today, few churches would call him to serve. But God had him serve everywhere! Paul was instrumental in laying the foundation of the church as Gentiles were grafted into God's family. This cute letter also reminds us that we shouldn't let the past hold us down. God wants to use us. We need to be ready, willing, and committed.

Unfortunately, some people are willing to serve God, but only as His consultant. They pray while they give God directions. They give of anything, but themselves. This is wrong.

Phillips Brooks simply points out the benefit of everyone serving, "Be such a man, and live such a life, that if every man were such as you, and every life a life like yours, this earth would be God's Paradise." From childhood we have heard "treat others the way you want to be treated." Edwin Hubbell Chapin said, "The creed of the true saint is to make the most of life, and to make the best of it."

We can benefit by remembering the words of Paul in Galatians 6:9: "Let us not become weary in doing good, for at the proper time we will reap a harvest if we do not give up." There may be times when service seems meaningless; however, we must press on. Service often implies *And Then Some*.

Luke 17:7-10 gives a practical illustration, "Suppose one of you had a servant plowing or looking after the sheep. Would he say to the servant when he comes in from the field, 'Come along now and sit down to eat'? Would he not rather say, 'Prepare my supper, get yourself ready and wait on me while I eat and drink; after that you may eat and drink'? Would he thank the servant because he did what he was told to do? So you also, when you have done everything you were told to do, should say, 'We are unworthy servants; we have only done our duty.'" We have failed if we only do enough to get by. We need to go over and above the call of duty in serving the Lord.

Most can relate to this concept of service when it comes to tipping at a restaurant. If the service has been mediocre, 10% is natural. If the service has been expected and good, 15% seems right; however, when the service is superb, people tip 20+% and may even give a positive comment to the manager. We appreciate service that is more than expected. God appreciates service that is *And Then Some*.

Matthew chapter 25 records the parable of the talents. Jesus tells the story of servants who were given 5, 2, and 1 talent. The servant who received only one talent didn't do anything with it and was considered wicked and lazy. However, the other servants doubled their talents. The response from the master was the same for both of them, "Well done, good and faithful servant! You have been faithful with a few things; I will put you in charge of many things. Come and share your master's happiness!" The ultimate prize will be to hear God say to us, "Well done, good and faithful servant!" Our aim should be service, not success.

Joshua closes his book with a clear challenge and statement of faith, "But if serving the LORD seems undesirable to you, then choose for yourselves this day whom you will serve, whether the gods your forefathers served beyond the River, or the gods of the Amorites, in whose land you are living. But as for me and my household, we will serve the LORD" (Joshua 24:15). The challenge is the same for today. We need to choose whether we will serve ourselves or the Lord. Hopefully, our choice will boldly be for the Lord.

Life is like a game of tennis; the player who serves well seldom loses.

CHAPTER FIVE - OUTWARD

US TO OTHERS

*"If someone forces you to go one mile,
go with him two mile."*
(Matthew 5:41).

Jesus set the example of living a life that typifies *And Then Some*. The natural response of a Christian would be to respond in like manner and return the favor. Finally, it should be realized that the believer's reaction must affect his interactions with others.

Jesus emphasized the importance of human treatment. Certain groups viewed Jesus as an enemy. In Matthew 22:34-39 they try to corner Him. When asked which of the hundreds of laws is most important, He is extremely straightforward: "Hearing that Jesus had silenced the Sadducees, the Pharisees got together. One of them, an expert in the law, tested him with this question: 'Teacher, which is the greatest commandment in the Law?' Jesus replied: 'Love the Lord your God with all your heart and with all your soul and with all your mind.' This is the first and greatest commandment. And the second is like it: 'Love your neighbor as yourself.'" Jesus had stumped the Sadducees. Now the Pharisees want a shot at Him. They asked Him a seemingly impossible question. Jesus replies to love God and to love your neighbor as yourself. In obeying Jesus, believers obviously must love God, but also love each other.

This passage is repeated in Mark chapter twelve and Luke chapter ten. The Scripture repeats this passage to get our attention. In case someone missed the point in Matthew, it is repeated in Mark. Realizing how slow, selfish and stubborn people can be, God gives us the story in Luke, too. After answering on how we are to love others, Jesus then goes into the story of the Good Samaritan. Being the great Teacher, Jesus follows His point with a clear, concise practical illustration. We should note; however, that loving God and our neighbors were commandments not suggestions. The previous section discussed serving Jesus directly. This section continues the thought of serving Jesus through others, like family, friends, enemies, and whoever crosses our paths.

1. Serve Jesus through others

Jesus surprised the masses in Matthew 25:34-40 when He pointed out that good deeds toward others are equal to serving Him, "Then the King will say to those on his right, 'Come, you who are blessed by my Father; take your inheritance, the kingdom prepared for you since the creation of the world. For I was hungry and you gave me something to eat, I was thirsty and you gave me something to drink, I was a stranger and you invited me in, I needed clothes and you clothed me, I was sick and you looked after me, I was in prison and you came to visit me.' Then the righteous will answer him, 'Lord, when did we see you hungry and feed you, or thirsty and give you something to drink? When did we see you a stranger and invite you in, or needing clothes and clothe you? When did we see you sick or in prison and go to visit you?' The King will reply, 'I tell you the truth, whatever you did for one of the least of these brothers of mine, you did for me.'"

It is humbling to realize that whatever we do for common folk, we are in essence doing for our Lord.

Henry Drummond hits the nail on the head when he said, "The greatest thing a man can do for his heavenly Father is to be kind to some of His other children." Recently,

a family expressed thanks to me in a gift that included flowers for my wife. That was so thoughtful. They realized that putting a smile on her face would touch my heart. It is the same way with God.

Perspective is everything. Motive motivates. Christopher Wren designed St. Paul's Cathedral in London. The cathedral is one of the world's most beautiful buildings. He wrote about the reactions of the construction workers who worked the job. The workers who appeared bored and tired answered that they were laying bricks or carrying stones. However, one worker was cheerful and enthusiastic as he mixed cement. When he was asked what he was doing, he said, "I'm building a magnificent cathedral." Perspective makes a world of difference. Paul reminds believers in Ephesians 6:7, "Serve wholeheartedly, as if you were serving the Lord, not men." To personally serve the Lord would be considered an honor. But, it is an honor we can partake of regularly through serving others.

Matthew recorded Jesus stating that when we serve others, we serve Him. However, Matthew also recorded Jesus stating the opposite realm. When we neglect others, we neglect Jesus. The younger generation may refer to this as "dis"ing someone. To neglect the needs of others is to "dis" the Lord Himself.

Matthew 25:41-45 continues Jesus' earlier lesson, "Then he will say to those on his left, 'Depart from me, you who are cursed, into the eternal fire prepared for the devil and his angels. For I was hungry and you gave me nothing to eat, I was thirsty and you gave me nothing to drink, I was a stranger and you did not invite me in, I needed clothes and you did not clothe me, I was sick and in prison and you did not look after me.' They also will answer, 'Lord, when did we see you hungry or thirsty or a stranger or needing clothes or sick or in prison, and did not help you?' He will reply, 'I tell you the truth, whatever you did not do for one of the least of these, you did not do for me.'" For us to see a need and ignore it is wrong. In fact, sin can be active or inactive action. James 4:17 says, "Anyone, then, who knows the good he ought to do and doesn't do it, sins."

Moses wrote in the book of Numbers specific regulations regarding life in general. Numbers 5:6 says, "Say to the Israelites: 'When a man or woman wrongs another in any way and so is unfaithful to the LORD, that person is guilty." The key point to be noted here is that when we do another wrong, we wrong the Lord. We end up being unfaithful to the Lord.

Joseph fully understood this principle. When he served in Potiphar's house, Potiphar's wife made a sexual advancement to him. This seemed to be an ongoing occurrence. Joseph declined every time. Finally, in Genesis 39:9 he says to Potiphar's wife, "No one is greater in this house than I am. My master has withheld nothing from me except you, because you are his wife. How then could I do such a wicked thing and sin against God?" Joseph knew that sinning against his master was actually sinning against his Master. To do a wrong to another is to do a wrong toward God Himself.

Everything comes back to love. The two greatest commandments are to love God and to love our neighbor as ourselves. John writes in 1 John 4:7-8, "Dear friends, let us love one another, for love comes from God. Everyone who loves has been born of God and knows God. Whoever does not love does not know God, because God is love." God is love. We love God when we love one another. Leo Tolstoy pointed out, "Where love is, there is God also." It appears the opposite may also be true.

An Irish Proverb states the following: "God likes help when helping people." It is such a privilege for us to be considered one of His helpers. Benjamin Franklin succinctly summarizes this mindset, "The most acceptable service of God is doing good to man."

2. Serve Jesus through family and friends

Service needs to start at home. Focus begins in the inner circle and works its way outward. Jesus' last recorded words on earth expressed this in Acts 1:8, "But you will receive power when the Holy Spirit comes on you; and you will be my witnesses in Jerusalem, and in all Judea and Samaria, and to the ends of the earth." Jesus directed the disciples to first start in their home town before they moved outward into the country and into the world.

In John 15:12 Jesus set the standard, "My command is this: Love each other as I have loved you." Serving family and friends requires love. Frank A. Clark pointed out, "A baby is born with a need to be loved – and never outgrows it." We need love. No matter what our age; we need to love and be loved. Further, our homes should typify love. We should look for opportunities to serve each other, knowing that service is nothing but love in work clothes.

Peter DeVries made a profound announcement, "We are not primarily put on this earth to see through one another, but to see one another through." All too often we try to over evaluate others. Such an attitude can definitely be called being judgmental. Love and service encourage one to be transparent, not to be one with x-ray vision into others' secret lives.

We are to love as Jesus loved. It is known that He came to serve, not to be served. EC McKenzie notes it is valuable to get to the point where one holds that "the measure of a man's greatness is not the number of servants he has, but the number of people he serves." He also observed that our actions are important because "love is more easily demonstrated than defined." People will always wonder how to define love. David Wilkerson pointed out, "Love is not only something you feel. It's something you do." In defining love, we should remember that it is not a feeling, but an action. We need to look for clever and fresh ways to serve our family and friends.

Paul repeated the thought in Galatians 5:14, "The entire law is summed up in a single command: "Love your neighbor as yourself." I am reminded that there are two kinds of people in the world: Givers and Takers. We need to be ones known for giving.

I received a beautiful gift a few years ago. In fact, it was one of the greatest gifts I have ever received as a speaker. A friend wrote me saying he had been praying daily for my upcoming speaking engagement. Not only that, but on Friday, the first day of the series, he would fast and pray three hours! That is serving *And Then Some*. I stepped to the platform with renewed confidence and purpose. I knew my

friend faced difficult times, yet reached out to me. Abraham Lincoln noted, "To ease another's heartache is to forget one's own." I experienced the phrase recorded by EC McKenzie "duty makes us do things well, but love makes us do them beautifully."

So, service involves love and giving. Edward Lindsey explained, "We think of a philanthropist as someone who donates big sums of money, yet the word is derived from two Greek words, philos (loving) and anthropos (man): loving man. All of us are capable of being philanthropists. We can give of ourselves." Service is giving love. We who love others are hence more philanthropists.

In John 13:34-35 Jesus said, "A new command I give you: Love one another. As I have loved you, so you must love one another. By this all men will know that you are my disciples, if you love one another." Jesus points out that love is the distinguishing feature of a true follower. And Lawrence Pearsall Jacks stated, "Nobody will know what you mean by saying that 'God is love' unless you act it as well."

C. Neil Strait pointed out this love in simple kindness, "Kindness is more than deeds. It is an attitude, an expression, a look, a touch. It is anything that lifts another person." Our goal should be to lift up someone else.

This is a practical experiment that can be quite challenging: If someone were to pay you $2 for every kind word you ever spoke and collect $1 for every unkind word, would you be rich or poor? Words can lift up or tear down. I appreciate the sentiment that is expressed through this poem:

Is anybody happier because you passed his way?

Does anyone remember that you spoke to him today?

This day is almost over, and its toiling time is through;

Is there anyone to utter now a friendly word for you?

Can you say tonight is passing with the days that slipped so fast,

That you helped a single person, of the many that you passed?

Is a single heart rejoicing over what you did or said?

Does one whose hopes were fading now with courage look ahead?

Did you waste the day, or lose it? Was it well or poorly spent?

Did you leave a trail of kindness or a scar of discontent?

Service starts in the home. The goal is to be a thermostat, not a thermometer. A thermometer tells temperature, and just adapts to the surroundings. When things get heated, its temperature rises also. A thermostat is different. This instrument changes and adjusts its surroundings. It sets the tone. When things get too hot, it cools them off. When the cold shoulder is apparent, it has a way of bringing warmth to the family.

3. Serve Jesus through enemies

Family, friends, and enemies often change clothes. Sometimes it feels difficult to know if someone is friend or foe. When it comes to service, we don't have to make a distinction. In Matthew 5:43-44 Jesus said, "You have heard that it was said, 'Love your neighbor and hate your enemy.' But I tell you: Love your enemies and pray for those who persecute you." We are to love our enemies. We are to serve our enemies.

This chapter opens with Matthew 5:41, "If someone forces you to go one mile, go with him two miles." This sounds kind of random for today, but in the first century this statement was very relevant. D. A. Carson studied the cultural situation. He points out that this "refers to the Roman practice of commandeering civilians to carry the luggage of military personnel a prescribed distance, one Roman 'mile.'" The Israelites were under Roman rule. A Roman soldier could boss an Israelite, and the Romans definitely practiced abuse. Jesus is radical when he says to go the extra mile. It would have been interesting to see the reaction of the soldier when he saw this Israelite servant keep on going past the mile mark. I believe that having a good attitude would also be implied. In 1 Corinthians 9:19 Paul strives to set the example,

"Though I am free and belong to no man, I make myself a slave to everyone, to win as many as possible." Serving others in love can lead to salvation. Martin Luther appears to be writing a commentary on this concept, "A Christian man is the most free lord of all, and subject to none; a Christian man is the most dutiful servant of all, and subject to everyone." He captured the essence of freedom in Christ while serving for Christ.

Remember, the difference between the ordinary and the extraordinary Christian lies in just three words: *And Then Some*. To serve loved ones is good, but to serve enemies is better - the next step.

The Golden Rule has been taught to children in Sunday School for years. I believe people miss how special Christianity is. Most other faiths have a Silver Rule; don't do to others what you don't want done to you. Parents commonly remind their child not to treat others in a way they wouldn't want to be treated. However, Christianity emphasizes the Golden Rule; do to others what you want done to you. We should not just practice passive tolerance, but add active kindness. Jesus tells us in Luke 6:31, "Do to others as you would have them do to you." Go for the gold!

The Book of Esther records a humorous occurrence. Haman is the King's right-hand man. Mordecai however is the one man he can't stand. One night the King can't sleep. He had his accomplishments read to him. He realizes that a man saved his life. He asks what he did to honor the man. He finds out that he forgot to honor him. At just this moment, Haman comes to the King's quarters to request the killing of Mordecai. The King asks Haman what he should do to honor someone very special. Haman thinks the King refers to him and suggests the royal treatment of ring, robe, horse and parade. The King then orders Haman to do this for Mordecai. Unintentionally, this story reflects how we as Christians should think daily. To observe The Golden Rule requires that believers treat their enemies the way they would want to be treated.

Typically, when someone does us wrong we want to practice one-upmanship. We don't really just want to get even, we want to one up them. As a believer, to truly go 'Over and Above' the call of duty involves forgiveness, respect and treating our enemy the way we would want to be spoiled.

One of the most famous passages of Scripture is Jesus washing the disciples' feet. John 13:2-7 records, "The evening meal was being served, and the devil had already prompted Judas Iscariot, son of Simon, to betray Jesus. Jesus knew that the Father had put all things under his power, and that he had come from God and was returning to God; so he got up from the meal, took off his outer clothing, and wrapped a towel around his waist. After that, he poured water into a basin and began to wash his disciples' feet, drying them with the towel that was wrapped around him. He came to Simon Peter, who said to him, 'Lord, are you going to wash my feet?' Jesus replied, 'You do not realize now what I am doing, but later you will understand.'" Message after message strives to capture the essence of Simon Peter's interaction with Jesus. In fact, sculptures even try to capture the moment. However, I believe an amazing point is missed. Jesus washed Judas' feet. Think about it. Jesus washed Judas' feet! Jesus, knowing that Judas would betray Him and lead Him to be tortured, to die, and something even worse – His Father turning away, washed Judas' feet. Jesus served His enemy. He washed his feet.

After that amazing display of humility, Jesus says in John 13:14-17, "Now that I, your Lord and Teacher, have washed your feet, you also should wash one another's feet. I have set you an example that you should do as I have done for you. I tell you the truth, no servant is greater than his master, nor is a messenger greater than the one who sent him. Now that you know these things, you will be blessed if you do them." Jesus set the example of humility. But even more,

He set the example of how to treat those who mistreat us. He washed his feet.

4. Serve Jesus through whoever crosses our paths

In Matthew 5:13-14 Jesus pointed out to all believers our responsibility, "You are the salt of the earth. But if the salt loses its saltiness, how can it be made salty again? It is no longer good for anything, except to be thrown out and trampled by men. You are the light of the world. A city on a hill cannot be hidden." Believers are the salt of the earth. We are to add spice to a bland world. Not only that, but believers are also the light of the world. In days full of darkness, we are to bring a glimmer of hope. We bring the light of direction.

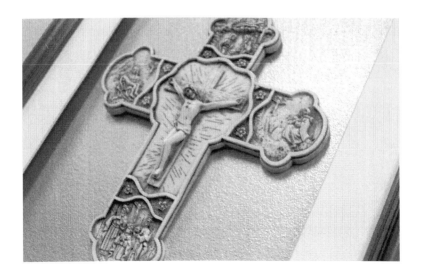

St. Augustine simply stated, "What does love look like? It has the hands to help others. It has the feet to hasten to the poor and needy. It has eyes to see misery and want. It has the ears to hear the sighs and sorrows of men. That is what love looks like." Love and service come out of a caring heart with active senses: looking, listening, feeling, tasting, smelling a better life for everyone and anyone.

I enjoy going to the YMCA and working out. I regularly take material, including drafts of this book, with me to read and edit in-between lifting repetitions. Lift thirty seconds, read thirty seconds, repeat. Work can also be accomplished while 'enjoying' the cardio machines. However, Lloyd Cory states, "the best exercise for strengthening the heart is reaching down and lifting people up." Helping others does the heart good.

There are at least four benefits we receive from serving others. First, serving others makes us feel good. Frank A. Clark said, "Kindness makes a fellow feel good whether it's being done to him or by him." This quote is so true. There are so many times I have gone to encourage someone else, and in the process, they lifted my spirits. Serving others feels good for both sides.

Second, serving others brings blessings. The Talmud says, "Whoever gives a small coin to a poor man has six blessings bestowed upon him, but he who speaks a kind word to him obtains eleven blessings." Matthew chapter five mentions that people who hunger and thirst for righteousness, who are merciful and pure in heart will be blessed by God. God doesn't miss a thing.

Third, serving others pleases God. Micah 6:8 states, "He has showed you, O man, what is good. And what does the LORD require of you? To act justly and to love mercy and to walk humbly with your God." Kindness pleases God. It fulfills God's expectations of us.

Fourth, serving others makes us good looking. Some translations of Proverbs 19:22 state that kindness makes one good looking. As a Youth Pastor, I would hear youth interact as they brought in their High school yearbooks. Routine phrases were repeated as the rating game began. Someone would say, "He (or she) is so hot!" The classmate would respond, "No, not if you knew them. But, check out this guy (or gal)." Regularly, people responded, "No way!" Again the classmate would respond, "Oh, if only you knew them." Kindness does make one more attractive.

Kindness needs to be something that we intentionally do. It doesn't just happen. In the story of the Good Samaritan, people intentionally went of their way not to help the needy individual, until, one stranger made a deliberate move to make a difference. Sometimes these actions are referred to as "Random Acts of Kindness." However, they are deliberately done for random individuals. We are to serve whomever our paths cross.

These random acts of kindness have no strings attached. Nothing is expected in return. St. Thomas Aquinas gave a simple example, "To love anyone is nothing else than to wish that person good." Other examples include:

> Pay for somebody's coffee (anonymously)
> Shovel someone's snow, cut their grass, bake something
> Give a smile, or a listening ear
> Driving – give up a close parking spot
> Shopping – give up your spot in line

Charles Kingsley challenged, "Make a rule, and pray to God to help you to keep it, never, if possible, to lie down at night without being able to say: 'I have made one human being at least a little wiser, or a little happier, or at least a little better this day.'" Stop and ask, "Am I making a difference in the world? Is it for the better or worse concerning others?"

John Wesley's personal mission statement can be partially summarized in his poem:

"Do all the good you can,
By all the means you can,
In all the ways you can,
In all the places you can,
At all the times you can,
To all the people you can,
As long as ever you can."

It is not too late

The difference between the ordinary and the extraordinary Christian lies in just three words: *And Then Some*.

It is not too late to change one's reputation. It is not too late to go from being ordinary to being extraordinary. One can still go from average to special. Wayne Rice illustrates this in a telling account.

Alfred Nobel made his fortune by inventing powerful explosives. He would sell the license to governments who would make war-changing weapons. When Alfred's brother died, the newspaper accidentally printed an obituary for Alfred. The writer identified Alfred as the inventor of dynamite who made a fortune by enabling armies with the ability for mass destruction. Alfred was bothered by what he would be remembered for. He decided to change his reputation. He took part of his wealth and established awards for accomplishments contributing to life rather than death. Today, when the name Nobel is mentioned, most people think of the peace prize, not explosives.

It is not too late to change one's reputation. Be extraordinary!

EC McKenzie recorded, "Kind words are short to speak, but their echoes are endless."

GOD
TO
US

US TO OTHERS

US
TO
GOD

CONCLUSION

THE SYMBOL

"Ask the LORD your God for a sign,
whether in the deepest depths
or in the highest heights"
(Isaiah 7:11).

The difference between the ordinary and the extraordinary Christian lies in just three words: *And Then Some.*

Marketing experts emphasize promotional logos, symbols, and designs. I thought it would be good to come up with a special symbol for *And Then Some.* I hoped for something to remind us that all our interactions need to be viewed from a new perspective.

God constantly gave His children visual reminders. The rainbow is painted across the sky after every rainfall as a precious reminder. After the Israelites crossed the Red Sea, they placed stones as visual reminders for generations to come. Even communion is designed as a reminder of Jesus and His work for us: "This is my body, which is for you; do this in remembrance of me" (1 Corinthians 11:24).

The WWJD (What Would Jesus Do?) bracelet touched so many lives. The bracelet was more than just a marketing tool. In fact, it became a way of life. When searching for a symbol for *And Then Some*, the most logical item that came to mind was the "plus sign." It would remind us to do more, to add a little special something, and to increase the giving of ourselves. Then I realized that symbol was already taken and well used. It is the cross! The whole concept of *And Then Some* goes back to where it all started, with God Himself.

This is an introduction to another book
by Dr. Johnson called LOST Lessons.

If you would like to purchase this book
plesae visit www.DrRandyJohnson.com.

LOST Lessons

Confused, isolated, and stranded; the survivors of Oceanic flight 815 are fighting to survive. In the midst of unknowns and mysteries; they are struggling to find their way, purpose and salvation. Many times in our Christian life we feel like this, we feel lost. We're confused, isolated and stranded; and just like the survivors, we are searching for direction. We struggle to grow close to God and live as He would want us. This book was written to help in this process. It uses the TV show LOST as a catalyst for thoughts, meditations and discussions of spiritual issues. It is designed as a devotional for young adults in hopes that it will be a tool used for spiritual growth. Each devotional contains a summary of a LOST episode highlighting a phrase, issue or theme, and then showing through Scripture how that concept relates to our Christian lives. LOST has changed lives in the area of entertainment, Jesus Christ changes lives today and forever. He offers abundant life (John 10:10) and everlasting life (John 3:16). The authors hope that reading this will encourage a meeting with the Author of life.

The authors in no way advocate or condone the content of the television show LOST; the show is rated at least TV14 and obviously is not suitable for all audiences. As with everything, caution should be used before or during viewing. The authors do not wish this book to be a stumbling block, but a benefit to a relationship with Christ. Do not partake in things that will hinder your walk with God. "Set your minds on things above, not on earthly things" (Colossians 3:2). Hopefully, this book will help you learn to view all of life from a heavenly perspective.

"NaRul DdaRaORa"

Oceanic flight 815 departs from Sydney, Australia and is scheduled to land in Los Angeles, California. While in flight, major complications occur; the plane splits in half and crashes on a tropical island. Only 48 survive. Blue waters, sandy beach and palm trees would normally be an ideal resort-like vacation, but today it is an unwanted detour. Jack, Kate and Charlie decide to go look for the cockpit, find the transceiver and actively seek rescue. As they are planning their mission, a Korean couple comes into view. The night is falling. It has been a long day. People are still scrambling. Uncertainty and fear are roaming throughout the survivors. Jin looks at his wife and says, "NaRul DdaRaORa." The closed caption reads, "Follow me." Is it that Jin was insecure and did not want to be alone? Or is he confident, loving and protective of his wife? The answer is not clear. Jin continues, "You must not leave my sight. You must follow me wherever I go." Dirty, scared, confused and still in shock, Sun nods in agreement. It appears they don't speak or understand English and none of the other survivors understand Korean. Therefore, they better stay together; there is no one else with whom they can communicate. One can feel all alone even though there are people all around him. Jin demands that Sun follow him.

Jesus often offered for others to, "Follow Me." Most immediately refused Him by ignoring His offer. To not answer is often to answer. In this case, by not saying yes with their feet, they were expressing rejection by standing still and saying nothing. Some refused by making excuses. One put Jesus off by wanting to wait until his father died (Luke 9:59). When his father finally dies, will he use the excuse that he has to care for his mother or run the family business? Maybe he was afraid that his father would disown him. This was a common punishment for those who left their Jewish upbringing. Whatever the reason for his excuse, by putting Jesus off he was saying, "No." Another put Jesus on hold by saying that he first wanted to go back and be sent off by his family (Luke 9:61). Family is important, but that delay was also a denial of Jesus' offer. Finally, one just looked away because he thought the offer was too costly (Mark 10:21). The offer may seem expensive, but to reject the Son of God leads to eternal bankruptcy.

However, a few took up His offer immediately. Levi (better known as Matthew) heeded His call, "After this, Jesus went out and saw a tax collector by the name of Levi sitting at his tax booth. 'Follow me,' Jesus said to him, and Levi got up, left everything and followed him" (Luke 5:27-28). Matthew had a job making good money; his life was probably very comfortable, and he had no apparent needs. Yet, at the calling of Jesus he followed. He wasn't concerned about his money or his booth. His only concern was to follow. Likewise, brothers Peter and Andrew jumped aboard, "As Jesus was walking beside the Sea of Galilee, he saw two brothers, Simon called Peter and his brother Andrew. They were casting a net into the lake, for they were fishermen. 'Come, follow me,' Jesus said, 'and I will make you fishers of men.' At once they left their nets and followed him" (Matthew 4:18-20). To leave one's nets behind sounds pretty definite. It would seem acceptable to first clean the nets and put them away, but the brothers chose a new direction in their lives at once. Matthew, Peter and Andrew immediately took up the charge to, "Follow Me."

Jesus extends the calling to all believers in Matthew 28:18-20: "Then Jesus came to them and said, 'All authority in heaven and on earth has been given to me. Therefore go and make disciples of all nations, baptizing them in the name of the Father and of the Son and of the Holy Spirit, and teaching them to obey everything I have commanded you. And surely I am with you always, to the very end of the age.'" Jesus invites all of us to follow Him.

What is God calling you to do today? _____

_____

_____

What gifts, talents and interests do you have and how could they be used for God? _____

_____

_____

_____

Have you considered going on a short term missions' trip?

_____

_____

Who has God placed in your life who doesn't know Him yet?

_____

_____

_____

What is your next step (invite them to church, give them a Christian book, share your story in a letter, email or verbally) and when will you do it? _____

_____

_____

_____

Jesus gives some basic ingredients for following Him daily, "Then he said to them all: 'If anyone would come after me, he must deny himself and take up his cross daily and follow me'" (Luke 9:23). Matthew left everything and followed Jesus. Peter and Andrew at once left everything and followed Jesus. They denied themselves and followed Him. Denying involves our talk and walk, our attitude and actions. Everyone is aware of Peter "denying" Jesus three times by Peter's claim to have had no association with Him (Luke 22:54-62). However, we miss Titus 1:16, "They claim to know God, but by their actions they deny him. They are detestable, disobedient and unfit for doing anything good."

Our words and actions are a testimony of who Jesus Christ is. We need to make sure it is a positive presentation.

Do your words and actions testify that you have taken the call to follow Jesus? _____

_____

What speaking sins (gossip, swearing, sexual innuendo, lying) do you need to eliminate from your life? _____

_____

_____

What sinful actions (stealing, alcohol, drugs, cheating) do you need to eliminate from your life? _____

_____

_____

As LOST goes on, we see that Sun battles with her choice as to whether or not she will wholeheartedly follow Jin. We need to stand firm with Joshua and announce, "As for me and my household, we will serve the LORD" (Joshua 24:15). I will follow Jesus!

"Every Trek Needs a Coward"

Jack, Kate and Charlie leave the other survivors on the beach as they look for the plane's cockpit. Upon arrival at the cockpit, Jack, Kate and Charlie find only the pilot alive. Almost immediately, a "monster" reaches through a broken window, grabs the pilot and kills him. Jack takes the transceiver and the three scouts frantically run for their lives while the monster comes after them. Charlie falls and gets his foot tangled on some vine. Jack comes back and frees Charlie's foot. In the panic the three get separated. Upon their reunion, Kate asks Charlie what he was doing back at the cockpit in the bathroom. Although he really went back for his heroin, he tells her that he was throwing up. Charlie then shamefully confesses, "Every trek needs a coward," and readily admits his fear.

Kate herself had faced fear only moments earlier. All alone in the dreaded woods her steps are frozen by fear. It was then she remembers Jack's approach to fear. While Kate was stitching a huge cut on Jack's back, Jack recounted facing fear early in his medical residency. He told how he gave fear 5 seconds to run its course and then he went back to work, and everything turned out fine. In the middle of the woods and fear, Kate counts,"1, 2, 3, 4, 5," and everything turned out fine.

Fear is a very active "monster." All too often we feed it our emotions and imagination. David had many Goliaths in his life, yet he appeared to have a secret ingredient. It is clear that a definite mindset on God is everything. In one of the most famous passages of all time, David writes, "Even though I walk through the valley of the shadow of death, I will fear no evil, for you are with me; your rod and your staff, they comfort me" (Psalm 23:4). As a shepherd boy David knew danger first hand. Sheep were a tasty treat for bears and lions. Yet, he had experienced God's deliverance from danger and fear. He fought the beasts with confidence and success. When David became an adult, fear was still near by. David ran for his life from King Saul and hid at En Gedi. This hide out had several caves built into the mountains on both sides of a valley. Saul and his mightiest men were after one man; David was the fugitive. The goal was not to bring him back alive. He was a wanted man, a wanted dead man. As David hid in the caves and peeked out, he truly looked at a valley of the shadow of death. But Psalm 42:1 shows David didn't see fear; he saw deer, "As the deer pants for streams of water, so my soul pants for you, O God." David's greatest goal was not to escape Saul, but to be found worthy by God. The closer the enemy came, the closer David sought to be to God. Fear didn't take him prey, it made him pray.

David didn't fear because he knew God was with him. Later he asks rhetorical questions, "The LORD is my light and my salvation — whom shall I fear? The LORD is the stronghold of my life — of whom shall I be afraid?" (Psalm 27:1) Knowing God means one doesn't really have to know fear. Finally, David gives a statement of triumph that we all want to encompass, "I sought the LORD, and he answered me; he delivered me from all my fears" (Psalm 34:4). That is an amazing declaration: the Lord delivered David from all his fears.

List three of your biggest fears. _____

_____

_____

_____

What would be the worst case scenario if your fears became reality? _____

_____

_____

People have a variety of fears today. Studies and anecdotal confessions show that public speaking may be fear number one for most people. However, private speaking to that someone special can be just as intimidating. When those communication encounters arise we need to remember that God wants to deliver us from all our fears. We are encouraged in 1 Peter 5:7: "Cast all your anxiety on him because he cares for you." We need to allow God into our daily lives with its fears as well as its victories. Paul gives clear direction when counting to five isn't enough, "Do not be anxious about anything, but in everything, by prayer and petition, with thanksgiving, present your requests to God. And the peace of God, which transcends all understanding, will guard your hearts and your minds in Christ Jesus" (Philippians 4:6-7). Prayer brings peace.

Do fears get in your way of being a witness for Christ? _____

_____

_____

What fear keeps you from witnessing more (rejection, being teased, not knowing the answer to a potential question)? __

_____

_____

Write out a prayer specifically asking God to strengthen your faith in Him and for deliverance from the fear. _____

_____

_____

_____

_____

I remember as a child fearing an open closet, a closed shower curtain, and "something" under the bed. With my heart beating I would run up the stairs fearing not only what was in the basement, but what might be under the stairs waiting to grab my ankle. However, fear disappeared when I was with my dad. My dad was my hero; he could conquer anything and definitely that certain "something." With age I have realized that my heavenly Father is always with me. This brings security, comfort and confidence. Every trek may need a coward, but God is willing to make sure it isn't one of His children. Fear Not!

"Everyone deserves a ..."

The Marshal is dying with a piece of shrapnel sticking out of his chest, yet frantically tries to warn Jack that some lady is dangerous. This seems to be a persistent concern when finally he tells Jack to check his jacket pocket. Jack finds a piece of paper that has a police mug shot of Kate. Kate is the dangerous woman. Kate is the fugitive. In the midst of all the drama, Kate has flashbacks of being in Australia. She remembers being on Ray's farm. When she finally left his farm, Ray pretended to drive her to the train station, but instead was turning her into the police for a $23,000 reward. He apologized and she understood. At that point he made a touching statement. He said, "Everyone deserves a fresh start." That is the theme and title of this episode: Tabula Rasa. It means clean slate. It is the idea of erasing a marker board totally clean, so it shines white as new, no marks or stains.

Episode three ends as Jack and Kate have a closing dialogue. Kate says, "I want to tell you what I did – why he was after me." However, Jack replies, "I don't want to know. It doesn't matter. Kate, who we were – what we did before this, before the crash. It doesn't really – 3 days ago we all died. We should all be able to start over." Everyone does deserve a fresh start.

God offers a fresh start. Acts chapter nine records the transformation of Saul, the persecutor of Christians, to Paul, the persecuted one for Christ. After the Lord's enlightening visit with Saul on the road to Damascus, God called on Ananias. This was not Ananias the high priest who belittled Paul (Acts 23-24). Nor was it the Ananias who lied to God, and along with his wife Sapphira, was struck down (Acts 5). They lied and died. No, this Ananias was different. He was open and honest with God. God told him that he was to go to the house of Judas and meet with Saul of Tarsus. In Acts 9:13-14 Ananias openly called to the Lord and said, "I have heard many reports about this man and all the harm he has done to your saints in Jerusalem. And he has come here with authority from the chief priests to arrest all who call on your name." It is almost as if Ananias expected the Lord to be surprised, to be unaware and to maybe even change His plans. Instead, God comforted Ananias by saying He had a special plan for Saul. Saul would suffer, but he was a chosen instrument by God. God forgave Saul and gave him a clean slate.

Paul shared his testimony in Acts 22:13. In describing Ananias' role, Paul said, "He stood beside me and said, 'Brother Saul, receive your sight!' And at that very moment I was able to see him." What a beautiful statement. It says that Ananias stood beside Paul. God forgave Paul and Ananias forgave Paul.

Matthew chapter eighteen contains what is often referred to as the Matthew 18 principle. If someone wrongs us we should first go directly to them. If repentance isn't present then we should take a witness. If the individual still chooses to live in sin we should take it to the church. The goal isn't church discipline; the goal is repentance, reconciliation and a fresh start. People all too often emphasize discipline (3 verses) and miss the emphasis on forgiveness (15 verses). Matthew 18:21-22 is clear that we need to continually forgive others (translated as 77 times in NIV, 490 times in KJV). It really isn't an option. We need to give them a fresh start and a clean slate.

Who has wronged you; who do you need to forgive? _____

_____

_____

_____

Pray asking God to help you forgive them and for wisdom to know how to stand beside them.

How should you now treat them? _____

_____

_____

It is difficult to forgive others; however, it is often even more difficult to forgive ourselves. First John 1:9 reminds us, "If we confess our sins, he is faithful and just and will forgive us our sins and purify us from all unrighteousness." God will forgive us. We need to accept His forgiveness. Jeremiah goes as far as to say that the Lord will forgive our sins and forget them (Jeremiah 31:34). He will not remember our sins. I like to think of a paper shredder as the forgiveness machine. My sin is like an IOU on a piece of paper. When I confess my sin to God, He takes the paper and puts it through the shredder. He will never use it against me; never rub it in my face. The IOU is eliminated.

Do you have unconfessed sin in your life? _____

_____

_____

Pray now asking God to forgive you and for wisdom to know how to turn from this sin in the future.

What plans can you now confidently pursue now that you have accepted God's forgiveness? _____

_____

_____

Micah paints a beautiful picture, "Who is a God like you, who pardons sin and forgives the transgression of the remnant of his inheritance? You do not stay angry forever but delight to show mercy. You will again have compassion on us; you will tread our sins underfoot and hurl all our iniquities into the depths of the sea" (Micah 7:18-19). The Lord forgives us and throws our sins into the deepest parts of the sea. We need to post a sign, "No fishing!" We need to accept God's forgiveness, leave the past alone and press on with a fresh start and a clean slate. God approves that everyone deserves a fresh start.

About the Author

Dr. Randy T. Johnson has been married to Angela for over 25 years. They have two children, Clint and Stephanie. He has been Chaplain and Bible teacher at Oakland Christian School in Auburn Hills, Michigan for about 20 years. He also ministers at two local Chinese Church youth groups. He co-authored *LOST Lessons* (a devotional based on the TV series LOST) and created *Read316.com* (an online program designed to quiz someone after they have read a section of Scripture).

For a complete list of the author's work go to
www.DrRandyJohnson.com

13846212R00079

Made in the USA
Charleston, SC
04 August 2012